Titchfield Ha

Birds
Day by Day

Compiled by Barry Duffin

Illustrations by Dan and Rosemary Powell

Published November 2009

Printed by Hampshire Printing Services, Winchester, Hampshire

The views expressed in this publication are not necessarily those held by the Hampshire County Council

Contents

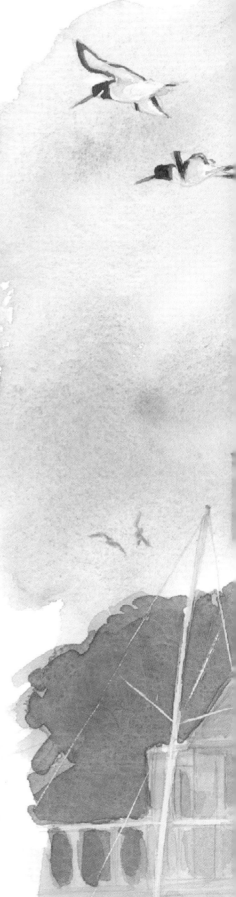

I am a regular visitor to Titchfield Haven and appreciate first hand the wealth of wildlife on view as well as the continued improvement of visitor facilities which enables everyone to enjoy this jewel in Hampshire's Crown.

In Hampshire we are fortunate in having one of the richest range of habitats found anywhere in lowland Britain - coastal saltmarshes and large estuarine systems, freshwater marshes and fen, ancient woodland, extensive heaths, valley mires, and chalk downland.

Over the last fifty years there has been a noticeable expansion in urban and industrial development in the county, which has put mounting pressure on our countryside. To counter this pressure a policy of protecting Hampshire's coast through acquisition was adopted by the County Council in 1972 resulting in the purchase of Titchfield Haven and subsequent areas of threatened habitats all along the coast. I am now proud to say that this ownership of a number of nature reserves, some of which are of outstanding ornithological importance, has guaranteed protection to a wide variety of habitats and their associated wildlife.

Since 1972 the sympathetic management by our Countryside Service staff, has brought about the recognition of this reserve as being one of the best examples of wetland management in the country, and one of the most popular sites for the visiting public in Hampshire.

I hope that this book will further encourage people to visit and enjoy Titchfield Haven and gain a better understanding of the wildlife to be seen there.

Margaret D Snaith - Tempia

Councillor Margaret Snaith-Tempia

HCC Executive Member
Culture and Recreation.

Foreword

Titchfield Haven has attracted bird-watchers for over half a century. My first visits to the reserve were in the early 1960s. In those days Dr Suffern led a small number of visitors on a short walk every Saturday and Sunday. Doc was a meticulous note-taker, something that he encouraged everyone to do. It is thanks to his notes, and those of the reserve staff and visitors, that publications like this are possible.

Memories of those early days are of an hour or two of a muddy walk up the eastern side of the Haven, with unfortunate disturbance, especially to birds on the river. That all changed in 1972 when Hampshire County Council acquired the reserve. The construction of hides and the provision of walkways resulted in the Haven becoming more accessible to visitors of all ages and the avoidance of the disturbance which was inevitable in the early days. The creation of the scrapes on the western side opened up a whole new area of the reserve to visitors and provided a valuable breeding, feeding and resting area for many species, especially wildfowl and waders. Coupled with this, water control measures steadily increased the area of reed-bed, providing more habitat for species such as Bittern, Marsh Harrier and Bearded Tit.

More recently, the acquisition of additional land by Hampshire County Council in the lower Meon Valley has created a larger sanctuary area for the wildlife and the provision of a first-rate visitor centre, with shop and tea-rooms, has encouraged appreciative visitors from far and wide.

I have personally witnessed the loss of some species from the reserve, such as breeding Common Snipe and Yellow Wagtail, but since the changes made by the County Council outlined above, I have also witnessed the arrival of several newcomers including breeding Avocet and Cetti's Warbler. It will be fascinating to relate the records in this book to the changes that have occurred over the years, not just in a local context, but also through the impact and influence of climate change that are clearly seen in this book.

Over the years many excellent photographs, drawings and paintings have been created by skilled visitors, volunteers and reserve staff. I am pleased to see that this book presents some of this work, providing an opportunity for a wider audience to appreciate them and the attraction of the reserve and its wildlife.

Richard Carpenter
Longstanding Volunteer

Introduction

'Titchfield Haven Birds Day by Day' brings to light a sample of just some of the highlights and facts among the many thousands of records associated with sightings of birds made at Titchfield Haven, many of which have never before appeared in previous publications.

With the opening up of the Haven to visitors in 1976, coupled with greater public interest in our environment and its wildlife, the contribution in sightings and the recording of the birdlife increased considerably. The number of daily reports logged nowadays dwarfs those made in the early twentieth century, with an estimated twenty thousand annual contributions now being made. There may have been far fewer contributors submitting reports of their observations in those early years but their records are viewed today as being of considerable value in illustrating and assessing the changes that have taken place since those days. Being one of the schoolboy enthusiasts who visited Titchfield Haven regularly at weekends from the beginning of January 1960, I did not hesitate in accepting the offer of the post of warden of the reserve in December 1972. In those early years after taking up my post I cannot over emphasize the importance I put on those past records of the birdlife of the area contributed by local naturalists. The notes made on the many species of birds associated with the site played a major part in formulating the initial plans for the creation of the reserve.

An entry in my diary for the 20th October 1962 states that two Cirl Buntings were observed in Marsh Lane fields. How was I to know at the time that this was to be the last known sighting of this species at the Haven. A few years later the Cirl Bunting, formerly a moderately common breeding bird in the Haven area, became extinct as a breeding bird in Hampshire. Nowadays with the availability of government agri-environmental schemes there may be opportunities in the future to realise the return of the Cirl Bunting as a resident in the county. Past information on distribution, population size and habitat requirements of the species will then aid the conservation of the species.

So a species was lost from the Haven, but in the short lifetime of the reserve a significant increase in the number of species of breeding birds has taken place. Many of these events are highlighted within this publication.

Barry Duffin
HCC Reserve Manager

Map of Reserve

Key

1 - Hill Head harbour	7 - Knocker's Orchard	13 - Water Meadows
2 - Meon Shore Hide	8 - Suffern Hide	14 - East Meadows
3 - Visitor Centre	9 - Spurgin Hide	15 - Knights Bank Hide
4 - Haven Cottage	10 - Eleven Acre Mere	16 - Marsh Lane
5 - North Scrape Hide	11 - Duck Bay	17 - Frying Pan
6 - Scrapes	12 - Meadow Hide	18 - West Meadows

19 - Mid-Marsh Reed-beds   Reserve Boundary ————
20 - Canal Path
21 - Upper Haven
22 - Posbrook Meadows
23 - Cooper's Marsh
24 - Posbrook Flood

January

January has traditionally been the time of year when the site has hosted the greatest numbers and variety of species of wildfowl. Almost forty species of ducks and geese have been recorded during the month, with Wigeon, Teal and Mallard being the most numerous. Nowadays with greater protection being given to the river valley and its flood meadows below Titchfield village wintering wildfowl can be viewed at close quarters, not only from the reserve's observation hides but also from the Titchfield canal path overlooking Posbrook Meadows.

An evening feeding station set up on the river close to Haven Cottage in the early 1980s, in order to starve wildfowlers of their quarry as they lined up on the reserve's northern boundary at dusk, may now attract over 500 duck at peak times. Not forgetting the importance of the coastal inshore waters and intertidal zone, offshore Great Crested Grebes gather off Brownwich cliffs, where shallow waters afford the birds an ideal roosting sanctuary from disturbance by fishing boats. The shingle spit at the mouth of the harbour can host Ringed Plover, Turnstones and other waders at high water if undisturbed.

1st The largest flock of **White-fronted Geese** recorded at the Haven is of 119 flying west on 1st January **1979** during a spell of cold weather.

2nd A male **Marsh Harrier** hunting over reed-beds opposite the Suffern hide on 2nd January **1996** was seen to drop into the reed-beds and then to carry off a **Water Rail**.

3rd The highest count of **Magpies** is of 82 on 3rd January **1986**. The majority of these birds were going to roost at Upper Haven.

On 3rd January **1990** a number of **Oystercatchers** among the roosting flock on the South Scrape showed traces of oil on their plumage, no doubt resulting from a spillage at the Fawley oil refinery the day before.

Two **Long-eared Owls** first discovered on 3rd January **1997** in willows behind the beach chalets remained until at least 14th March.

At least 300 **Kittiwakes** moved westwards offshore on 3rd January **1998**.

East meadows from the Meadow Hide in winter 1996 (Barry Duffin)

4th A drake **Shoveler** ringed on 4th January **1984** was shot 3134 km to the north-east in Archangel, Russia on 15th May 1984.

Drake Shoveler on South Scrape (Barry Duffin)

On the 4th January **1998** three **Great Skuas** were offshore whilst a fourth rested on the beach.

5th A flock of 18 **Yellowhammers** was found feeding in a stubble field alongside the canal on 5th January **1985**.

6th In force ten, gusting eleven westerly winds in the late morning of 6th January **1988**, two **Little Auks** and a **Leach's Petrel** flew east offshore, whilst another **Leach's Petrel** flew in over the scrapes. Late in the day another **Little Auk** that had been picked up earlier in a road in Lee-on-the-Solent was released successfully.

7th An immature **Marsh Harrier** was watched collecting sticks and reeds and then dropping them into the reed-beds on 7th January **2001**.

8th The largest wintering number of **Common Scoter** is of a flock of 120 offshore on 8th January **1966**.

A **Brent Goose** of the pale-bellied race *Branta bernicla hrota* was observed feeding in the estuary at low water on 8th January **1979**.

9th The highest count of **Turnstones** is of 154 on the South Scrape on 9th January **1977**.

10th A **Blackbird** ringed at the Haven on 10th January **1979,** was found dead 1001 km to the east in Germany on 14th June 1979.

11th The first **Jack Snipe** to be identified at the Haven was on 11th January **1953**.

A **Hooded Crow** flying southwest on 11th January **1960** was only the third record of this rare winter visitor.

12th An exceptional gathering of 10 **Red-necked Grebes** occurred offshore from 12th-19th January **1957**.

The largest winter gathering of **Coot** is of 500 on 12th January **1964**. The birds were feeding in the east meadows close to the Frying Pan.

On 12th January **1987**, after a night when the temperature fell to -8.9°C and few areas of water remained unfrozen 94 **Shovelers** were counted, of which 80 were feeding in the estuary.

River Meon in December 1978 from the Suffern hide (Barry Duffin)

13th Two **Ruddy Ducks** first appearing on 13th January **1982**, were joined by others during the month with a maximum of 6 drakes and 6 ducks from 17th to 19th. A single duck remained until 31st January. Also observed on 13th January **1982** during cold weather were 8 **Red-crested Pochard** offshore. The flock which included 6 drakes was thought to have been displaced from the Netherlands by cold weather.

The highest count of **Pochard** at the Haven was on 13th January **1996** when 204 duck came in to the evening feeding station.

14th During a cold weather movement of passerines on 14th January **1960** some 33,000 **Skylarks** were counted flying north-west.

One of the highest counts of **Smew** is of 10 from 14th January **1963** to 16th March 1963 during severe weather.

An immature **Great Black-backed Gull** was witnessed taking a **Tufted Duck** off the water in the lower reaches of the river on 14th January **2004**.

15th The largest gathering of **Great Black-backed Gulls** is of 370 on the shore at low water on 15th January **1960**.

A flock of 23 **Waxwings** was observed flying west over Posbrook on 15th January 1966.

16th Twelve **Bewick's Swans** frequented the reserve and adjoining farmland from 16th January to 28th February **1987**. During this cold weather period the swans were fed potatoes and wheat put out on the scrapes.

Bewick's Swans in Old Street fields February 1987 (Dennis Bright)

At dusk on 16th January **1987** in falling temperatures, 3,300 **Wigeon** were counted flighting westwards out of the reserve and onto nearby farmland to feed overnight on autumn sown cereals. This was a record number for the site.

17th A party of 8 **Goosanders**, including 3 drakes, was on the river on 17th January **1985**.

A female **Snow Bunting** located on the beach at 1250 hrs on 17th January **1986** later flew north up the valley.

18th During severe winter weather on 18th January **1963** a **Woodcock** flew in from the sea onto Hill Head beach where it was caught by a local cat.

On the 18th January **1985**, during extreme cold weather, a **Water Rail** was observed drowning a Meadow Pipit on the edge of the canal. The rail stood on the pipit holding it underwater. Eventually the pipit was lifted out of the water and the rail ran off into the undergrowth with it.

19th The first **Pink-footed Geese** recorded in Hampshire was of a flock of 24 flying north at the Haven on 19th January **1946**.

The first occurrence of **Iceland Gull** at the Haven was of a first winter bird on 19th January **1984**. This bird was shortly followed by another on 22nd, with one of these birds remaining until 27th March. A third first winter bird was found on 27th February, whilst an adult was noted in early February up until 18th of that month. Unprecedented numbers occurred in the British Isles in the latter half of January.

A **Bittern** found crouching on a snowy slope in the shelter of a hedge on 19th January **1985** was later picked up and taken into care. The bird was successfully released two days later after being fed sprats delivered on the end of a three foot long litterpicker. Fitting a yellow colour ring on the bird's leg enabled it to be identified out on the marsh on 17th February.

Bittern January 19th 1985
(Barry Duffin)

20th A drake **Green-winged Teal** was observed from the Meadow hide on 20th and 21st January **1990**.

21st A **Storm Petrel** was discovered on the Frying Pan at 1030 hrs on 21st January **1980**. The bird left two hours later, being seen to lift into the air during force nine southwesterly winds and a hailstorm, and was last seen heading inland.

22nd A large flock of **Tree Sparrows** feeding in a field of kale from December 1961 until April 1962, reached a peak of 750 birds on 22nd January **1962**.

23rd Two **Long-eared Owls** were flushed from sallows close to the southwest boundary dyke on 23rd January **1986**. At least one was still in the same area the next day.

Long-eared Owl January 1986 (Barry Duffin)

24th During a period of severe cold weather a **Redwing** was trapped on 24th January **1979** and was found to have been ringed earlier that month on 3rd January, at Tring in Hertfordshire.

25th A drake **Teal** ringed on 25th January **1984** was recaptured at the Haven in February 1985, again in December 1985 and finally was shot 2168 km to the north-east in northern Finland on 20th September 1987. This illustrates a faithfulness to wintering sites of this species, with this bird most probably having spent at least three winters at the Haven and no doubt was returning for a fourth before being hunted.

26th An adult drake **Teal** ringed at the Haven on 26th January **1987,** was shot 2154 km to the north-east in the St.Petersburg district of Russia on 28th August 1989.

27th During severe winter weather and icing over of the river 308 **Tufted Ducks** were counted on 27th January **1963** in a single raft offshore.

The highest day count of wintering **Common Snipe** is of 500 on 27th January **1975**.

17

28th Forty-three **Shelducks** came in to the evening feeding station at Haven Cottage on 28th January 1992.

*Shelduck drake
(Barry Duffin)*

29th One of the largest flocks of **Velvet Scoters** is of 21 flying east during severe cold weather on 29th January 1956.

On 29th January 1987 a **Long-tailed Skua** in sub-adult plumage circled over the Haven at 1000 hrs before heading off in a north-easterly direction. The sixth Hampshire record.

30th The leg and ring of an adult **Moorhen** ringed at the reserve on 8th January 1982 were found on 30th January 1989 574 km to the east in the Netherlands. An interesting recovery of a species considered to be mainly a resident at the Haven.

31st At least 60 **Redwings** were feeding on fallen apples in Knocker's Orchard on 31st January 1996.

February

Despite warmer winters, southern England can still experience short periods of cold weather, particularly during the month of February. It is during these times when plunging overnight temperatures may continue during daylight hours, presenting harsh feeding conditions for some of the reserve's resident birds. The Cetti's Warbler population that depends on the ability to forage for insects and other invertebrates close to the ground or water's edge, can be vulnerable on these occasions.

The icing over of the river margins and adjoining reed-beds can often result in Water Rails and Common Snipe being forced out into the open in search of food. Among the most favoured haunts of the rails are edges of the reed-beds opposite the roadside viewing platform and the area below the Meon Shore hide.

In the event of overnight snowfalls, coastal movements of large numbers of passerines might be witnessed as they flee badly affected areas in search of open, unfrozen ground. The seawall at Hill Head can be a good vantage point for the observer on these occasions as mixed flocks of thrushes, larks and finches may move along the coast both over the sea and inland over the marshes.

1st The highest count of **Bean Geese** in the County is of a flock of 15 that flew into the reserve at 1500 hrs on 1st February **1976**, and settled with the grazing **Wigeon** flock. These birds continued to frequent the eastern meadows until 8th February, with 6 remaining until 15th February.

2nd A **Coot** was heard circling high over Haven Cottage and the river at 1800 hrs on 2nd February **2006**. The bird was calling repeatedly. This habit has been recorded often in February and March with individuals frequently heading off eastwards.

3rd The highest winter count of **Tufted Ducks** is of 300 during severe weather on 3rd February **1963**. The majority of these birds spent time on the sea when the river was iced over.

4th A Hampshire record gathering of 220 **Great Crested Grebes** was offshore on 4th February **1996**.

The largest flock of **Greylag Geese** is of 29 flying down river and then off along the coast in a westerly direction on 4th February **2003**.

5th A male **Hen Harrier** was hunting over the upper valley reed-beds at dusk on 5th February **2003**.

6th On the 6th February **1986** after a light covering of snow in the early hours, and frequent snow flurries during the remainder of the day, an easterly movement of passerines was witnessed. Large numbers of thrushes and larks were involved. In six hours watching 14,114 **Fieldfares**, 9,669 **Redwings** and 2,038 **Skylarks** were counted. Four **Woodlarks** were also observed during this movement, one of which sang briefly whilst in flight. In addition a **Lapland Bunting** alighted briefly on the seafront before almost immediately flying back westwards.

Wigeon flock in east meadows (Barry Duffin)

A second winter plumage **Iceland Gull** that arrived on the river on 6th February **2004** remained in the area until at least 11th March.

Second winter Iceland Gull from Suffern Hide February 2004 (Barry Duffin)

7th The highest count of **Scaup** is of 21, including 10 drakes, on the sea off Hill Head on 7th February **1997**.

8th A wintering flock of **Ruff** reached a peak of 105 birds on 8th February **1977**.

9th At least 30 **Coot** corpses were found along the shore on 9th February **1963** as a result of prolonged cold weather.

The wintering flock of **Curlew** reached a peak of 153 on 9th February **1993**.

10th With the river iced over for several days and after a night when the temperature fell to -8°C, six **Woodcock** were flushed from alongside the eastern boardwalk on 10th February **1991**.

11th On the morning of 11th February **2005** a **Bittern** was observed from the Meadow Hide as it flew into the pond below the hide from across the meadows. It was reported to have taken a Great Crested Newt.

12th On the 12th February **1989** a **Raven** was observed flying down river and out to sea towards the Isle of Wight. This was the first record for the Haven.

13th A **Green-winged Teal** came in with a flock of **Teal** to feed on food put out in the evening in front of the Suffern hide on 13th February **1991**, on a day when river ice began breaking up.

14th An unusually pale plumage **Stonechat** was feeding along with others in a recently cut reed-bed on 14th February **1983**.

Stonechat February 1983 (Ingrid Duffin)

15th A **Pomarine Skua** offshore on 15th February **2003** was only the second record for that month.

16th A female **Little Bunting** was trapped and ringed on 16th February **1992**. This was only the second occurrence in Hampshire of this eastern vagrant. The bird remained until at least 17th April.

17th A minimum of thirteen **Wrens** were counted leaving an old nest under the eaves of Haven Cottage early on the morning of 17th February **1979**.

The highest count of **Moorhens** is of 179 on 17th February **1984**.

18th The earliest return date for the breeding **Avocets** has been of 6 birds on 18th February **2008**.

19th The highest count of wintering **Black-tailed Godwits** is of 1,450 on 19th February **1985**, at a time when extensive flooding occurred in the valley below Titchfield village.

Black-tailed Godwit flock over east meadows (Dennis Bright)

Ruff attracted to wheat put out for wintering wildfowl on the lawn at Haven Cottage during cold weather, peaked at 24 birds on 19th February **1991**.

20th A male **Reed Bunting** retrapped on 20th February **1986**, had been ringed on 28th October 1984 in Belgium, 354 km to the east.

21st The largest flock of **White-fronted Geese** is of sixty-seven on 21st February **1981**. The birds were observed flighting in from the north-west and then veering off eastwards.

22nd In severe cold weather at the beginning of **1963** six **Short-eared Owls** were observed in the air together after being flushed from the upper marshes on 22nd February. Four of these birds remained until at least the 4th March.

The highest ever count of **Pintail** is of 29, including 21 drakes, on 22nd February **2005**. The duck were attracted to flooded meadows in the upper reserve.

23rd A **Grey Phalarope** on the sea on 23rd February **1996** was the latest ever winter date in the County, and only the second ever for the month of February.

24th A **Coot** identified by its colour ring on the 24th February **1984**, had been ringed in St.James Park London on 10th November 1982.

A **Pochard** ringed on 24th February **1986** was shot near Moscow on 20th August 1988, 2752 km to the east.

25th The autumn of 2008 saw for the first time in over twenty years **House Sparrows** taking up residence in the grounds of Haven Cottage and the visitor centre. By the 25th February **2009** the small population had reached at least twenty birds.

26th The highest count of **Great Northern Divers** on a single day is of 4 offshore on 26th February **1955**.

Posbrook Meadows in flood February 1990 (Barry Duffin)

27th A pair of **Common Cranes** flew into the reserve from a northerly direction on 27th February **1979**, and settled on the western meadows at a range of three hundred metres from the observers in failing light.

28th Four **Bean Geese** present on 28th February and 1st March **1981** was only the third occurrence on the reserve.

29th A **Spoonbill** first observed on 29th February **2000** remained until 12th March.

March

The first spring migrants are arriving, particularly on fine days with light winds when Meadow Pipits and Sand Martins can be seen coming in from the south. By night flocks of Common Gulls and Curlews, heading for their Scandinavian breeding grounds can be heard moving over eastwards on occasions.

Within the reserve Cetti's Warblers are now in full song as well as newly arrived Chiffchaffs. Towards the end of the month the first Willow Warblers may be arriving along with Blackcaps. Other migrants such as Wheatears are most likely to be found on the clifftop fields to the west of the reserve.

On the scrapes the calls of recently arrived Avocets are now to be heard whilst the aerial display of lapwings is a delight to see. Black-tailed Godwits that have spent the winter on the reserve are beginning to get their colourful summer plumage, shortly to be leaving for their Icelandic breeding grounds. Other long distance travellers about to leave our shores are the Brent Geese. Several hundred will be feeding daily in the estuary at low water.

1st At least 25 **Water Pipits** were feeding in meadows close to the canal path on 1st March **1996**.

2nd A **Bittern** was watched feeding in the pond below the Meadow hide during the late afternoon of 2nd March **1997**.

3rd A first winter **Iceland Gull** was present on the shore on 3rd March **1993**.

4th Seven **Grey Herons** were catching frogs in the pond below the Meadow hide on 4th March **1992**.

Grey Heron (Dennis Bright)

5th The earliest spring record of **Garganey** is of a pair on 5th March **1977**.

6th The earliest spring **Wheatear** was on 6th March **1977**.

On 6th March **1995** a female **Blackcap** that had been ringed at the Haven as an adult in September 1990, was found dead in snow in Morocco, 1743 km to the south.

7th At 0957 hrs on 7th March **1993**, whilst in Haven Cottage, the calling of wild swans was heard. Exiting the cottage at speed brought the rewarding sight of a large flock of low flying **Bewick's Swans** overhead, heading in a north-easterly direction. In the short time the birds were in view an estimated 70 individuals were involved. It was highly likely that these birds were from the wintering Avon Valley flock, and the beginning of their spring migration back to the Siberian breeding grounds was being witnessed. Earlier in the day presumably the same flock were reported over the Lower Test Marshes and then at Dibden Bay at 0930 hrs.

8th A drake **Ring-necked Duck** discovered on the river on 8th March **1996** remained until 26th. This was the first record for the Haven of this North American duck. During its stay some of the best views of the bird by visiting birders were from the kitchen window of Haven Cottage.

9th An adult **Whooper Swan** was picked up dead on 9th March **1974**. This bird had last been seen alive on 26th February. One of a pair of Whooper Swans that had previously been on the reserve until 9th February and thereafter at Alresford Pond, was found in a sick state at the pond in early February. The loss of these two birds brought to an end six years of this small wintering flock at the reserve.

10th Over 50 **Reed Buntings** were coming to feed on millet put out at Haven Cottage on 10th March **1988**.

Male Reed Bunting March 1988 (Dennis Bright)

11th The earliest spring **Swallow** is of a single bird on 11th March **1994**.

12th Three **Sand Martins** on 12th March 2003 was the second earliest record for the Haven. The earliest having been on 11th March **1957**.

13th On the morning of 13th March **1960** an escaped South American **Puna Teal** flew onto the river as observers walked towards the Frying Pan.

14th A **Gannet** found dead on the tideline on 14th March **2003** had been ringed as a chick in a nest on Alderney, Channel Islands on 22nd June 1996.

15th A count of 12 **Jack Snipe** on 15th March **1957** is the second highest spring total for the County.

The first record of **Long-eared Owls** at the Haven was of two birds discovered on 15th March **1976**. One of these birds remained until at least 28th March.

A **Red-legged Partridge** was observed on the morning of 15th March **1981** perched on the seawall of all places.

16th The earliest **White Wagtail** was present on 16th March **2000**.

17th A **Red Kite** first observed from the harbour bridge soaring high over the scrapes at 1235 hrs on 17th March **1986**, eventually flapped slowly off westwards pursued by two **Carrion Crows**. Earlier that morning a male **Brambling** was in full song at Upper Haven.

18th The first occurrence of a **Green-winged Teal** in Hampshire was of a drake found in the company of **Teal** at the Haven on 18th March **1956**.

One of the earliest records of a spring **Willow Warbler** was on 18th March **1992**.

19th On the 19th March **1961** Britain's first **Cetti's Warbler** was trapped in reeds close to the harbour bridge. The bird had first been observed on 4th March, but its identity was not confirmed until it was later caught. It remained in the area until at least 10th April.

20th The earliest ever **Arctic Skua** in Hampshire was offshore from the Haven on 20th March **1979**. The bird was also present the next day.

21st The earliest spring **Sedge Warbler** was recorded on 21st March **1957**.

22nd The earliest spring sighting of a **Ring Ouzel** is on 22nd March **1953**.

23rd Flocks of migrating **Curlews** and **Common Gulls** were heard moving eastwards over the lower Haven at 11.30pm on 23rd March **1996**.

24th Migrating **Curlew** moving east over the reserve on 24th March **1976** were joined by birds leaving the meadows.

The earliest spring **Common Sandpiper** recorded on the reserve is of a single bird on 24th March **1995**.

25th A s many as 815 **Meadow Pipits** were counted coming in off the sea during the course of the morning on 25th March **1987**.

The earliest records of **House Martin** have been of single birds on 25th March **1988** and **1992**.

26th An **Alpine Swift** which had spent the night roosting in an office of the General Register Office building outside Titchfield, was released at Titchfield Haven on 26th March **1990** after being fed mealworms.

Alpine Swift 26th March 1990
(Ingrid Duffin)

A **Hoopoe** was observed flying towards Hammond's Bridge on the Titchfield canal on the morning of 26th March **1989**. It was later located feeding on a farm tip to the west of the bridge.

27th Four **Black-necked Grebes** in full summer plumage were offshore on 27th March **1983**.

28th A **Mute Swan** found dead along the canal on 28th March **1986** had been ringed almost sixteen years earlier at Emsworth, West Sussex on 9th April **1970**.

29th The Haven's first spring **Bluethroat** was found on the east bank of the South Scrape in the evening on 29th March **1998**. The bird was of the white-spotted race. This was the fourth record for the Haven.

30th An early nesting pair of **Blackbirds** were feeding young close to Haven Cottage on 30th March **1977**.

31st A number of decoy wooden **Black-headed Gulls** were put out on the South Scrape on 31st March **1981** with the aim of attracting breeding birds. At least one of the decoys was convincing enough to be identified as a Mediterranean Gull by a visiting member of the county council's staff, who subsequently featured this sighting in his regular newspaper 'nature notes' article.

Posbrook Meadows and Hollom Hill Farm (Barry Duffin)

The Haven from the west August 1989 (Barry Duffin)

Wintering Lapwing over the eastern meadows February 1975 (Barry Duffin)

32

April

At a time when the spring migration is getting into full swing, a stroll along the canal path can often be rewarding to view newly arrived passerines such as Whitethroats, Lesser Whitethroats and perhaps the first Cuckoo. Usually it is not until the second week of the month that Reed and Sedge Warblers are likely to be heard in the reed-beds.

By mid month nest building by several hundred pairs of Black-headed Gulls on the scrapes is well under way, as vegetation cut the previous autumn is put to good use. In recent years flocks of Mediterranean Gulls have been putting in regular appearances, being attracted by the activity of their near relatives.

At sea the first terns are likely to be seen, particularly Sandwich Terns. Light southerly winds will bring in Swallows and Sand Martins as well as the occasional Yellow Wagtail.

1st On the 1st April **1981** flocks of **Common Gulls** passed over the Haven during the evening. From 1930 hrs to 2000 hrs some 250 birds were witnessed heading eastwards at some height, in large 'V' formations. The movement continued after dark with very vocal flocks passing overhead.

The earliest **Common Terns** recorded havebeen of 5 offshore on 1st April **1999**.

2nd The earliest recorded spring **Lesser Whitethroat** is of one on 2nd April **1992**.

3rd An immature **Cormorant** was found dead on the riverside on 3rd April **1981** with an extremely large eel that it had partly swallowed.

A **Willow Warbler** ringed at the Haven on 13th August 1998 was retrapped on the island of Menorca, Spain, on 3rd April **1999**.

4th A **Bittern** was reported to have been heard booming on 4th April **1929**.

Unprecedented numbers of **Mediterranean Gulls** were present on the reserve in April **2008**. The highest single day count was of 320 on the scrapes on 4th.

Mediterranean Gulls on the Scrapes April 2008 (Barry Duffin)

5th A **Great Crested Grebe** picked up from the shore on 5th April **2006** had two fishing hooks and line removed before being released.

Great Crested Grebe being released after the removal of fishing hooks April 2006
(Caroline Brickwood)

6th The highest count of **Yellowhammers** is of 80+ birds feeding in a newly sown field alongside Upper Haven on 6th April **1974**.

7th One of the largest spring passage movements of **Kittiwakes** ever witnessed off the coast of Hampshire is of 553 birds flying east offshore on 7th April **1979**.

Three **Common Cranes** flew over the lower Haven at 1450 hrs on 7th April **1984** in a westerly direction.

8th The early appearance of 3 **Common Swifts** on 8th April **1997** has only been equalled once since in Hampshire.

A **Cuckoo** on 8th April **1969** remains the earliest on record at the Haven.

9th The earliest spring dates for **Grasshopper Warbler** have been on 9th April, in the years **1981** and **1982**.

10th A **Slavonian Grebe** in full summer plumage was offshore on 10th April **1979**.

11th The earliest **Black Tern** records for the Haven, and indeed for Hampshire, have been of a single bird on 11th April **1966** and of 2 on 11th April **1979**.

12th During the evening of 12th April **1984**, at approximately 2045 hrs, five **Little Grebes** left the river from in front of the Suffern hide and flew down river gaining height as they reached the seawall before veering off eastwards over the Solent. Prior to putting to flight the birds were noted displaying with fluffing of feathers, bathing and neck stretching. They often swam close together, frequently turning to face into the south-westerly breeze. The suggestion is that these were wintering birds witnessed leaving for breeding sites to the east, maybe as far as the Continent.

A summer plumage **Black-necked Grebe** discovered offshore on 12th April **1994**, remained in the area until 17th April.

13th Over 3000 **Black-headed Gulls** were present on the scrapes on the evening of 13th April **2008**.

View across South Scrape towards Suffern Hide April 2008 (Barry Duffin)

14th The earliest recorded spring **Wood Warbler** is of one singing on 14th April **1956**.

A flock of 103 **Kittiwakes** fed offshore from approximately 1830 hrs for an hour on 14th April **1984**, before gradually moving off eastwards.

Male Dartford Warbler (Dennis Bright)

A **Dartford Warbler** was in full song at the lower end of the Haven in roadside gorse on 14th April **2008**.

15th A **Common Crane** was observed on farmland to the west of the reserve at 0900 hrs on 15th April **1991**. The sixth record for the reserve.

16th Hampshire's first ever record of **Richard's Pipits** was of 2 at the Haven on 16th April **1955**.

The earliest spring **Turtle Dove** recorded was observed on the western boundary of the reserve on 16th April **1989**.

17th A pair of **Black-winged Stilts** spent the day feeding on the South Scrape on 17th April **2002**. This brought the total recorded in the County to 20.

18th The highest spring count of **Ruff** is of 32 flying north-east up river on 18th April **1981**.

19th On the evening of 19th April **1974** observers counted 150 **Curlew** moving east. This is the highest day total for spring passage in Hampshire.

20th A **Green-winged Teal** from 19th to 20th April **1997** was the fourteenth record for Hampshire.

During a large easterly seabird passage on 20th April **1999** 79 **Little Gulls** were counted.

The first breeding record of **Greylag Goose** was in **2007** when a pair with 5 goslings was observed on 20th April.

21st In **1977** a reed-bed roost of 350 **Sand Martins** was recorded on 21st April, one of the largest spring roost recorded in Hampshire.

A recently arrived migrant **Tree Pipit** was singing on 21st April **1986** from the tops of hawthorn bushes on the western edge of the water meadows.

22nd A late drake **Goosander** was on the river from 22nd until 24th April **2005**.

The Scrapes from the Meon Shore hide April 2007 (Barry Duffin)

23rd A **Surf Scoter** observed on the sea at 0908 hrs on 23rd April **1999** along with two **Common Scoters**, later flew off eastwards. The three birds had been observed off Hurst Beach at 0834 hrs that same day. This was only the second Hampshire record.

24th The first occurrence of **Collared Dove** in the Haven area was of a single bird on 24th April **1963**. The bird was in a garden of a house in Old Street.

A **Caspian Tern** found resting on the shore on 24th April **1995** at 1655 hrs, flew off westwards twenty minutes later. This was only the second record for Hampshire.

25th The highest spring count of **Velvet Scoters** is of 20 offshore on 25th April **1981**.

26th On 26th April **1982** a **Magpie** was seen to land on the lawn of Haven Cottage and almost immediately proceed to decapitate a recently fledged Blackbird.

A **Hobby** was observed on the evening of 26th April **1983** taking an unidentified bat over the copse on the western boundary of the reserve.

27th A **Common Crane** first observed gliding in over the scrapes from the southwest in the early afternoon of 27th April **1984,** gradually gained height and soared out over the sea until lost into the sun. This was the fourth record for the reserve.

There have been few double figure counts of spring migrating **Arctic Terns**. One of the largest flocks identified however is of 33 flying north up the valley on 27th April **1991**.

28th The highest spring count of **Greenshanks** is of a flock of 19 that arrived from the west at 0824 hrs on 28th April **1987**. The birds remained feeding in the lower river for several hours.

A migrant **Wood Sandpiper** was in full song when displaying over the scrapes on 28th April **1996**.

29th A period of moderate easterly winds at the end of April **1984** brought one of the largest spring passage movements of **Bar-tailed Godwits** ever witnessed. From the early hours on 29th April flocks moved offshore in an easterly direction. This spring passage movement continued throughout the day until dusk with a temporary lull in mid-afternoon. By the end of the day 3,689 birds had been counted, whilst the overall total for the last week of April amounted to over 7,200.

A **Reed Warbler** ringed at the Haven on 21st August 1981, was subsequently retrapped in Portugal on 20th August 1983, and once again on 29th April **1984** on the Cherbourg peninsula in France.

30th A **Black Kite** was watched over the canal path before flying off in a north-westerly direction on 30th April **1998**.

May

Early in the month large numbers of seabirds may be witnessed passing offshore in an easterly direction. The most spectacular movements often take place when fast moving depressions pass through the English Channel. The resulting weather pattern can be strong south-easterly winds accompanied by rain and poor visibility. In these conditions birds are funnelled into the Solent and can be observed at close quarters if watching from the seawall.

This diurnal passage is often dominated by flocks of Common and Sandwich Terns, and Bar-tailed Godwits, with smaller numbers of Whimbrel, Little Terns, Sanderling and Dunlin. On occasions Black Terns can be involved, whilst Arctic Skuas are frequently seen pursuing and harassing the migrating terns.

Newly arrived Common Swifts can be seen almost daily hawking for insects throughout the valley, being forced to feed at low levels in inclement weather. May is often the best month to look out for Hobbies feeding high over the upper reserve on warm days. In recent years up to 6 birds have been recorded on a single day.

Pochard gathering at the evening feeding station (Barry Duffin)

Nesting Black-headed Gulls April 2008 (Barry Duffin)

1st A **Spoonbill** flew north up the valley until out of sight on 1st May **1998**.

2nd An adult **Purple Heron** was flushed from the waterside at 1730 hrs on 2nd May **2007** whilst a nearby bank was being mown by a tractor. This was only the third record for the reserve.

The highest day count of **Little Egrets** is of 20 on 2nd May **2007**.

3rd On 3rd May **1980** 850 **Swallows** were counted arriving from the south between 1000 hrs and 1300 hrs. Also that day 97 **Yellow Wagtails** were counted coming in from the south during the morning, the highest Hampshire spring day total.

Thirty-two adult **Avocets** on 3rd May **2007** is the highest number ever recorded at the Haven.

Avocets on the South Scrape May 2008 (Dennis Bright)

4th The first **Mediterranean Gull** to occur at the Haven was a single bird on 4th May **1968**.

On the 4th May **1983** a sub-adult **Purple Heron** was seen to fly off westwards from the Haven. This was the first occurrence at the Haven.

Three **Temminck's Stints** were present on the scrapes from 4th to 6th May **2000**.

43

5th The first record of a **Red Kite** at the Haven was on 5th May **1974**.

On the 5th May **1985** 26 **Arctic Skuas** were observed moving eastwards during a large seabird passage.

A **Wood Warbler** was singing from within Knocker's Orchard close to the east boundary on 5th May **1988**.

A drake **Green-winged Teal** first found feeding on the North Scrape on 5th May **1989,** remained until at least 28th May.

6th A total of 64 **Shelducks** flew east during a spring seabird passage on 6th May **1976**.

A **Lesser Flamingo** was present on the scrapes on the evening of 6th May **1988**.

Lesser Flamingo over South Scrape May 1988 (Dennis Bright)

A **Water Pipit** on 6th May **1998** is the latest spring record for the species in Hampshire.

7th The arrival of 1,256 **Common Swifts** in from the Solent on 7th May **1981** is the largest spring immigration ever witnessed, as is the arrival of 300 **House Martins** on the same day.

An **American Wigeon** that was present from 7th May **1987** remained until 19th July 1987. The fourth record for Hampshire.

A **Fieldfare** on 7th May **1991** in front of the Meadow Hide has been the latest spring record.

On 7th May **2000** a **Spotted Crake** was heard calling from Haven Cottage in calm conditions just after midnight.

A **Hobby** hunting over the western meadows was observed taking a white budgerigar in flight after a brief chase during the morning of 7th May **2000**.

8th The highest count of **Mute Swans** is of 80 on 8th May **2000**.

Mute Swan and young (Barry Duffin)

9th An escaped **Chinese Blue Magpie** was observed along the eastern boundary hedgerow on 9th May **1978**.

On the evening of 9th May **1984** 350 **Whimbrel** were counted moving east between 1600 hrs and 1830 hrs, including a single flock of 125 birds. This is the highest ever day count of spring passage birds in Hampshire.

10th A **Temminck's Stint** on the scrapes on 10th May **1993** was the ninety-ninth for Hampshire. The bird remained until 12th.

During the night of 10th May **1993** a **Sedge Warbler** that had been ringed at the Haven the previous August, was found dead on Bardsey Island after hitting the lighthouse, as a result of being dazzled by the beams of light.

11th The largest spring passage of **Black Terns** is of 173 flying east on 11th May **1960**.

The first **Savi's Warbler** to be recorded in Hampshire was a male that held territory at the Haven from 11th May to 21st June **1969**, but it was considered not to have attracted a mate.

12th The largest gathering of **Shelducks** is of 80 on 12th May **1984**.

A **Great Reed Warbler** was singing in the evening on 12th May **2001** from a reed-bed on the boundary of Upper and Lower Haven. This is only the second Haven record of this species and the seventh for Hampshire.

On the evening of 12th May **2004** a flock of 9 **Pomarine Skuas** was watched offshore. Eventually the birds moved off eastwards.

13th A **Common Swift** taken in flight by a Sparrowhawk on 13th May **1981** was dropped onto the path leading to the North Scrape hide.

The largest recorded brood of **Shoveler** ducklings is of eleven on 13th May **2007**.

A **Quail** was observed on 13th May **2009** flying across the east meadows after being flushed by a Magpie. Only the fourth record for the Haven.

14th An adult **Night Heron** was discovered in riverside willows at Cooper's Marsh on 14th May **1990**. This was the first record for the Haven.

15th A drake **Shoveler** ringed at the Haven on 4th January **1984,** was shot later in the year on 15th May 3134 km to the north-east near the White Sea port of Archangel. No doubt this bird was close to its breeding grounds at this time of year.

16th Four **Wood Sandpipers** on 16th May **1961** was the highest spring count in the County of this species, until it was equalled at the Lower Test in 1992.

A **Bittern** was heard booming on 16th May **1970**.

17th Two **Manx Shearwaters** observed offshore on 17th May **1979** eventually flew up Southampton Water.

One of two **Pomarine Skuas** observed offshore on 17th May **1984** perched on a piece of driftwood. The two birds later flew up Southampton Water.

18th A **Great Reed Warbler** first seen on 18th May **1960** remained until 24th May. This was the third Hampshire record and the first for the Haven.

During an early morning breeding census on the 18th May **1981**, an adult male **Little Bittern** was found perching in riverside willows. This was the seventh bird to have been recorded at the Haven out of a Hampshire total of eleven since 1953.

19th A pair of **Kingfishers** were observed entering a possible nesting site on 19th May **1968**.

20th After a day of southerly gale-force winds and heavy rain showers on 20th May **1986**, a first summer **Gannet** was found storm driven on the beach.

A **Whiskered Tern** put in a brief appearance on the South Scrape on 20th May **2005**. The bird remained long enough for it to be photographed whilst perched on posts and rails close to the Meon Shore hide. This was the first occurrence for the reserve and the sixth record for Hampshire.

Whiskered Tern and Sandwich Tern South Scrape 20th May 2005
(Ted Pressey)

21st Two **Little Bitterns** were observed on 21st and 22nd May **1960**, with one remaining until 26th May. This was the third occurrence of this rare vagrant at the Haven.

Around midday on 21st May **1999** two **Kentish Plovers** were identified on the shore. Later in the afternoon presumably one of the same two birds, a female, was discovered feeding on the South Scrape. This bird remained until 24th May. This was only the sixth record for the Haven.

River Meon from Haven Cottage (Barry Duffin)

Late records of **Short-eared Owls** have been of single birds on 21st and 28th May **2003**.

A **Red-rumped Swallow** observed on 21st May **2006** was only the fourth accepted record for the County.

22nd The first sighting of an **Avocet** at the Haven was when a flock of 4 appeared on 22nd May **1948**.

A **Slavonian Grebe** offshore on 22nd May **1959** is the latest ever record for Hampshire.

An adult female **Pectoral Sandpiper** was present on the North Scrape between 1945 and 2015 hrs on 22nd May **1991**. This was presumably the same bird as that observed at Warsash the previous day. The bird remained until late evening of the following day when it was then seen flying off northwards. The third spring record for Hampshire.

23rd A pair of **Great Crested Grebes** with 3 newly hatched young observed on 23rd May **2007** was the first breeding success for this species at the Haven.

24th A **Common Buzzard** was observed taking a week old Avocet chick on the evening of 24th May **2008**. The bird stood on a mudbank for half an hour waiting for chicks to come out from cover, before pouncing. This bird was ultimately responsible for predating large numbers of gull and wader chicks.

Common Buzzard mobbed by gulls over Scrapes May 2008 (Barry Duffin)

25th A **Marsh Warbler** was in full song when discovered on 25th May **1992**. It remained in the locality until at least 15th June. This was the fourth record for the reserve.

26th At 0500 hrs on 26th May **1988** a **Marsh Warbler** was singing close to the harbour bridge and later on at least two occasions in the grounds of Haven Cottage. This was the second occurrence at the Haven of this rare summer visitor.

The first spring record of a **Honey Buzzard** was on 26th May **1999** when a single bird flew west at 1300 hrs.

49

An adult **Gull-billed Tern** was discovered flying over the South Scrape at 0810 hrs on 26th May **2003**. The bird remained until 0850 hrs before flying off westwards. This was the thirteenth record for Hampshire.

Although often suspected, it was not until 26th May **2005** that **Shoveler** were proved to have bred, when a duck was observed accompanied by a brood of nine young.

27th In the late afternoon on 27th May **1989** an **Osprey** was observed above the Suffern hide carrying a fish. The bird eventually flew out to sea after being continually mobbed by a crow. Presumably the same bird returned to fish the river daily until 31st of the month, often resting on a dead tree near the Frying Pan.

A **Long-tailed Duck** last seen offshore on 27th May **2000** had been present since 7th May. This is the latest ever County spring record.

28th A **Great Northern Diver** offshore on 28th May **2002** was one of the latest ever in the County.

In thick fog on the morning of 28th May **2003** a male **Golden Oriole** was singing from an alder outside Haven Cottage at 0635 hrs.

29th A **Little Egret** on 29th May **1960** was only the third Hampshire record and the first for the Haven.

A **Magpie** was observed carrying off a **Moorhen** chick from the South Scrape on 29th May **1983**.

The third occurrence of a **Marsh Warbler** at the Haven was a bird found singing close to the canal towpath at 0530 hrs on 29th May **1989**.

30th Whilst carrying out a spring breeding bird census on 30th May **2001** a **Bluethroat** was found singing in the reed-marsh at Upper Haven. This was the fifth record for the Haven.

31st A **Little Egret** on 31st May **1979** was only the third record for the reserve.

June

The breeding season is in full swing, with the scrapes being a focal point for a wide range of species. Nesting Black-headed Gulls are present in their hundreds, with many pairs having young near to fledging, whilst late-comers may still be on eggs. Close examination of the colony and the scarcer Mediterranean Gull is likely to be located.

The scrapes not only provide ideal sanctuary for a wide range of breeding birds at this time of year, but can attract feeding flocks of summering Black-tailed Godwits and a high tide roost of non-breeding Oystercatchers.

Early in the month newly fledged Cetti's Warbler young can be heard in undergrowth alongside the visitor paths but it is only the patient observer who will chance on a glimpse of this elusive warbler. There is a better chance however of viewing Kingfishers on the river. Having bred to the north of the reserve both adults and young will travel down the Meon from mid-month onwards and are regularly observed fishing from posts or reed stems opposite the Suffern hide.

1st At approximately 1050 hrs on 1st June **2002** a **Red Kite** was observed flying south over the east meadows.

Two **Oystercatchers** were discovered sitting on nests within rows of cultivated strawberries just west of the reserve on 1st June **2007**.

2nd One of the largest flocks of **Long-tailed Tits** recorded is of 21 on 2nd June **1971**.

The latest ever Hampshire **Black-throated Diver** was offshore on 2nd June **1987**.

3rd The first breeding record of **Canada Goose** was in **1976** when a pair with two goslings were present on 3rd June.

Two **Bee-eaters** were observed close to the North Scrape hide briefly on 3rd June **2005** before flying on up the valley. This was the eleventh Hampshire record.

Looking south from the Suffern hide August 1989 (Barry Duffin)

4th At 1425 hrs on 4th June **1995** an **Alpine Swift** was observed over the eastern boundary. This was the sixth Hampshire record of this species.

5th A **Nightjar** that had flown into workshops in Portsmouth Naval Dockyard on 5th June **1993** was released at the Haven unharmed two days later.

A male **Red-backed Shrike** present for the day on 5th June **1996**, was only the sixth occurrence at the Haven of this scarce migrant.

During strong winds and squally showers on 5th June **2008**, the nest of a pair of **Great Crested Grebes** drifted down river as chicks were only just hatching. One chick survived.

6th A **Glossy Ibis** was observed from the canal path in flooded meadows in the upper reserve on 6th June **1977**. This was the first record for the Haven and the fourth for Hampshire.

7th A pair of **Cetti's Warblers** feeding recently fledged young on 7th June **1981** was the first proof of breeding at the Haven.

At least 500 **Common Terns** were feeding offshore on 7th June **1991** together with several hundred **Black-headed Gulls**. Large numbers of fish were inshore feeding on shoals of whitebait that were leaping onto the tide-line at times to escape the larger fish.

8th A **Wood Warbler** ringed as a nestling in Gloucestershire on 8th June **2001** was retrapped at the Haven on 3rd August 2001.

Wood Warbler
August 2001
(Barry Duffin)

Offshore Eider flock (Dennis Bright)

The largest summering flock of **Eider** is of 40 offshore on 8th June **2003**.

9th An adult **Little Bittern** was observed at the lower end of the river at 0945 hrs on 9th June **1968**. This was the sixth bird recorded at the Haven since the first for Hampshire in 1953.

An adult female **Red-necked Phalarope** found on the South Scrape at 1230 hrs on 9th June **1982** remained until the evening, when it flew off in a north-easterly direction with Redshanks.

10th The largest summering flock of **Common Scoters** is of 34 offshore on 10th June **2009**.

11th The largest number of **Shelduck** ducklings recorded is of eighteen on 11th June **2004**.

12th The longest staying **Spoonbill** is an adult that arrived on 12th June **1989** and remained until 1st September.

13th An adult male **Little Bittern** was seen to fly from reeds close to the harbour bridge and across the river at 1130 hrs on 13th June **1954**. The bird was present the following day in the same area. This was the second occurrence at the Haven and the second Hampshire record.

On 13th June **1993** a male **Red-backed Shrike** was watched along the canal path for forty-five minutes before it flew off up the Haven. The third Haven record.

54

14th A **Marsh Warbler** was singing on the west side of the reserve on 14th June **1988** at 4.50am, and again later at 6.30am. The bird was observed as it perched on hemlock water-dropwort plants whilst singing. This may have been the bird recorded earlier in the month when found singing on the east side of the reserve.

15th A **Siskin** observed flying south on 15th June **1993** was an unusual date for the site. The only **Marsh Tit** to have been ringed at the Haven was also on 15th June **1993**.

A **Black-headed Gull** ringed in Lithuania on 15th June **2000**, was found dead on the shore at Hill Head on 1st December 2001, 1721 km to the west of the ringing site.

16th The first **Little-ringed Plover** chick to be hatched on the reserve was observed on 16th June **1984**. This was a welcome surprise as the day before the nest had been predated by a Coot, and all eggs were thought to have been lost.

The first **Marsh Warbler** to occur at the Haven was a bird found in full song, singing from riverside sallows at 0530 hrs on 16th June **1987**.

17th A female **Teal** was flushed off a nest in the base of a bramble patch close to the east boundary on 17th June **1991**.

On 17th June **2001** an adult **Redshank** that had hatched 3 chicks early in the afternoon was denied access to them when an **Oystercatcher** took over the brooding. The Oystercatcher in question had lost its own young recently.

18th A **Marsh Tit** on 18th June **2000** was only the third occurrence at the Haven in the month of June.

The Lower Haven June 2004 (Barry Duffin)

Avocet with newly hatched chick South Scrape (Dennis Bright)

19th The reserve's first ever **Avocet** chick was hatched on 19th June **2004**.

20th A party of recently fledged **Goldcrests** were being fed by two adults in the lower branches of pine trees not far from the visitor centre on 20th June **1996**.

21st A record number of 18 **Avocet** chicks present on 21st June **2006** later fledged successfully.

Mistle Thrushes are by no means a common bird in the area, but a party of 8 was feeding in a rhubarb crop close to the reserve's west boundary on 21st June **2009**.

22nd The first ever breeding pair of **Oystercatchers** on the reserve hatched a single chick on 22nd June **1988**. The same day the finding of a brood of **Tufted Duck** ducklings was the first proof of breeding of this species on the reserve.

A **Curlew Sandpiper** on 22nd June **1992** was only the second spring record for the reserve.

A drake **Eider** was discovered on the morning of 22nd June **2003** hanging from a timber groyne on a dropping tide. The bird had been snared by hook and fishing line, as well as an extremely large lead weight. A successful release followed.

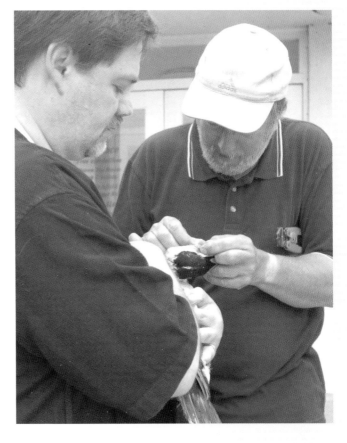

Fishing hook being removed from a drake Eider June 2003 (Rosemary Powell)

23rd The first occurrence of **Manx Shearwaters** off the Haven was of 5 flying south-west on 23rd June **1958**.

A reed-bed roost of some 2,200 **Starlings** on 23rd June **1985** was made up of predominantly juvenile birds.

24th In the early afternoon of 24th June **2002** attention was drawn to Hill Head harbour where a pair of **Avocets** were discovered mobbing pedestrians and passing cars. On further investigation two **Avocet** chicks were found stranded below the harbour wall. They were carried around to the scrapes, at head height with the adults in pursuit, and released. Both chicks fledged two weeks later. Following disturbance on the breeding site at Warsash the adults had walked the chicks to Hill Head earlier in the day. Both chicks were ringed prior to release into the scrapes and one of these birds was subsequently found breeding in the Netherlands on 25th May 2005. This was only the third occurrence of a British ringed **Avocet** being found in the Netherlands.

Avocet chicks Hill Head harbour June 2002 (Barry Duffin)

Avocet chicks after being rescued June 2002 (Barry Duffin)

Avocet and young on North Scrape (Barry Duffin)

25th A nesting pair of **Common Terns** on the South Scrape on 25th June **1977** were unfortunately not successful in rearing young. This was however the first breeding attempt on the reserve.

26th An adult and a first summer **Spoonbill** arrived on 26th June **1989**. Both birds stayed in the area until early September when the adult departed whilst the first summer bird remained until 20th September. The latter bird that carried identifiable colour rings had been ringed in a nest at Terschelling, Netherlands in 1988.

Immature Spoonbill from Suffern Hide 1989 (Dennis Bright)

27th On the evening of 27th June **1996** at least 25 juvenile **Bearded Tits** were together in the reed-bed across the river from the Suffern hide.

28th A juvenile **Great Spotted Woodpecker** found dead at Hedge End on 28th June **1991**, had been ringed at the Haven ten days earlier.

29th It is unusual to see a **Great Spotted Woodpecker** flying over large expanses of water on the south coast, so a bird arriving from the direction of the Isle of Wight on 29th June **1981** was surprising.

30th A female **Teal** with five ducklings was on the river just north of the Frying Pan on 30th June **1978**. The adult bird, squawking loudly, circled a dinghy from where observations were being made. This remains the only record of Teal rearing young on the reserve.

Spring Shrikes sketched 1996 and 2002

July

Early July sees the beginning of the return migration for many northern breeding waders such as, Green Sandpiper, Turnstone, Common Sandpiper and Greenshank, whilst many of the reserve's summer visitors Common Terns, Reed and Sedge Warblers included, may still be feeding young in the nest. On the scrapes broods of Mallard, Shelduck, Shoveler and Gadwall are well grown but yet to fledge.

By the third week of the month Sand Martins are much in evidence. Overnight roosting birds leave the reed-beds at dawn and head out southwards across the Solent, at a time when the first autumn nocturnal migrants are dropping in on their journey south. Whitethroats, Sedge Warblers and Willow Warblers can be among the most noticeable species involved at the beginning of this exodus, along with Grasshopper Warblers that may be in equal abundance but are hardly noticeable.

July is probably one of the best months to observe small parties of Gannets offshore, particularly if there are spells of strong winds. There may also be a number of summering Common Scoter or Eider at sea.

1st A flock of over a thousand **Starlings** circled low over the river for about twenty minutes at dusks on 1st July **1980**, before going to roost for the night in nearby reed-beds.

2nd The first proof of breeding **Gadwall** was obtained on 2nd July **1989** when a brood of three young was noted.

3rd A female **Kentish Plover** was on the South Scrape briefly on 3rd July **1999**.

4th Two **Grasshopper Warblers** were in full song at Upper Haven on 4th July **1981**, whilst nearby three newly fledged young were flushed from low vegetation.

5th An **Egyptian Goose** that arrived on the 5th July **2004** remained in the area until the end of June 2005. During the 2005 breeding season this bird was extremely aggressive towards breeding birds on the scrapes, and was responsible for destroying the nests of many birds including that of a pair of Avocets.

6th A newly fledged **Savi's Warbler** was trapped and ringed on 6th July **1978**. This was the first confirmed breeding record in Hampshire.

7th Broods of 5 and 4 nestling **Sparrowhawks** were ringed at the Haven on 7th July **1992** and 7th July **1993**. Of these nine young birds four were known to have died as a consequence of hitting window panes. Two from the 1992 brood of all females died within six weeks of fledging, one in Petworth, Sussex and the other in Warsash. The two others from the 1993 nest of all males, died in East Cowes, Isle of Wight in March 1995, and Hill Head in August 1994.

A **Squacco Heron** that was discovered in the reed-beds to the north of the scrapes on 7th July **1994** remained for a further two days. This was the second Hampshire record of this rare heron.

8th On the afternoon of 8th July **2006** a **Kestrel** flew into the garden of the visitor centre closely pursued by a noisy **Common Tern**. It was immediately realised that the falcon was carrying a tern chick. Seconds later the Kestrel was flushed from underneath a picnic table, where it dropped the chick. Having found that the chick had received only superficial injuries it was returned to its nesting platform in the river.

9th By the end of June the majority of **Cuckoos** have normally stopped calling. However hearing one on 9th July **1991** was a particularly late date.

Cuckoo (Dennis Bright)

The first proof of breeding **Mediterranean Gulls** at the Haven was when a recently hatched chick was observed on 9th July **2006**.

10th The evening of 10th July **1990** was the first time in a fortnight that winds had dropped enough to visit a site in mid marsh where a **Savi's Warbler** had been singing previously. The bird was clearly heard between 8pm and 9.30pm.

11th An estimated 700 **Common Swifts** were hawking for insects over the marshes during the evening on 11th July **2000**.

12th A **Bittern** was showing frequently in flight on 12th July **2000** as it made several short flights crossing the river close to the Suffern Hide.

13th A pair of **Bearded Tits** caught on 6th November 1986 had both been ringed as juveniles at Stodmarsh, Kent on 13th July **1985**.

14th A **Puffin** was found dead on Hill Head shore on 14th July **1957**. There have only been two further records since this date.

The longevity record for a **Cetti's Warbler** ringed on the reserve is 4 years 3 months and 23 days. The bird was an adult female first ringed on 14th July **1999**.

Cetti's Warbler (Barry Duffin)

15th A late singing **Grasshopper Warbler** was recorded in the water meadows on 15th July **2008**.

16th A **Tawny Owl** was hooting down the chimney of Haven Cottage at 10pm on 16th July **2000**.

17th The highest count of summering **Black-tailed Godwits** is of 175 on the scrapes on 17th July **2008**.

A **Kestrel** ringed as a nestling at Itchen Stoke on 17th July **1989,** was retrapped 30 km to the south at the Haven on 2nd September 1989.

18th The first **Red-backed Shrike** to be recorded at the Haven was a male on 18th July **1962**.

19th A **Bearded Tit** ringed at the Haven on 23rd December 1992 was retrapped at Stodmarsh in Kent, 179 km to the east, on 19th July **1994**.

The highest count of **Gannets** offshore is of 45 on 19th July **2008**.

20th A scarce visitor to the reserve was a **Lesser Spotted Woodpecker**, observed in trees close to Haven Cottage on 20th July **1992**.

21st Four broods of recently fledged **Avocets** arrived on the scrapes accompanied by adults on 21st July **2008**.

22nd A recently fledged **Cuckoo** observed close to the North Scrape hide, was probably being fed by a nearby **Reed Warbler** on 22nd July 1986.

23rd The five hundredth **Cetti's Warbler** to be ringed at the Haven was on 23rd July **2005**.

24th The first Hampshire record of **Roseate Tern** was of 4 flying up the valley on 24th July **1955**. The Haven remains the most reliable site in the County to observe this species during the month of July.

The first **Common Tern** chick to hatch at the Haven was on 24th July **1994**. The bird fledged successfully.

25th The first record of a **Rose-ringed Parakeet** was on 25th July **1982**.

In **1993** a **Rock Pipit** present from 25th July onwards was the earliest returning bird on record for the reserve.

26th A **Temminck's Stint** present on the scrapes on 26th and 27th July **1976** was frequently observed giving display flight.

A **Bee-eater** was observed from the harbour bridge as it flew inland on 26th July **2001**. The eighth record for Hampshire.

A particularly early catch of **Grasshopper Warblers** was of 20 on 26th July **2008**.

Grasshopper Warbler (Barry Duffin)

65

27th On the 27th July **1975** an estimated 6,000 **Black-headed Gulls** were observed hawking for insects over the marshes, whilst a further 1,800 were in the Haven. This has been so far the largest gathering of this species at the reserve.

Seven **Roseate Terns** were observed among a flock of 250 **Common Terns** resting on the beach below the yacht-club on 27th July **2004**. This is the highest single count on record for the reserve.

28th A **White-rumped Sandpiper** found on the South Scrape on 28th July **1999**, remained until 3rd August. The fourth record for the reserve.

29th The only **Willow Tit** to have been ringed at the Haven was on 29th July **1981**.

A total of 1150 **Common Terns** were counted resting on the shore at low water on 29th July **2007**.

Common Terns Hill Head shore July 2007 (Barry Duffin)

30th Two **Yellow-legged Gulls** were observed on the shore among other gulls on 30th July **1993**.

31st A **Curlew Sandpiper** in full breeding plumage was present on the scrapes on 31st July **1983**.

August

The autumn migration is now in full swing. Early morning can bring large arrivals of nocturnal migrants, with the peak of the Willow Warbler migration occurring in the first ten days of the month. Whilst Whitethroats and Garden Warblers are more likely to be seen feeding in hedgerows along the canal path and in patches of bramble close to the coast road, it is the grazing meadows where Wheatears and Whinchats may be found feeding. Yellow Wagtails are often observed in the latter half of the month among grazing cattle. Towards dusk an observer standing on the harbour bridge or on the nearby public viewing platform may be treated to the spectacle of the wagtails going to roost in the reed-beds across the river. Flocking Swallows and Sand Martins may also join the wagtails before dropping into the reeds where they will spend the night.

During the day flocks of several hundred Common Terns may be seen fishing offshore, whilst others periodically rest at low water on the shore close to the yacht-club. Both Roseate and Black Terns can frequently be found among these gatherings.

1st A **Spotted Crake** was showing well in front of the Spurgin hide for long periods on the afternoon of 1st August **1993**.

2nd On 2nd August **1990** during hot anticyclonic weather with light south-easterly winds 100 **Black Terns** drifted into the Haven and the immediate shore area from the Solent. All the birds were considered to be adults.

3rd A **Mediterranean Shearwater** was observed offshore between 1630 and 1900 hrs on 3rd August **1994**. This was the fifth record for Hampshire.

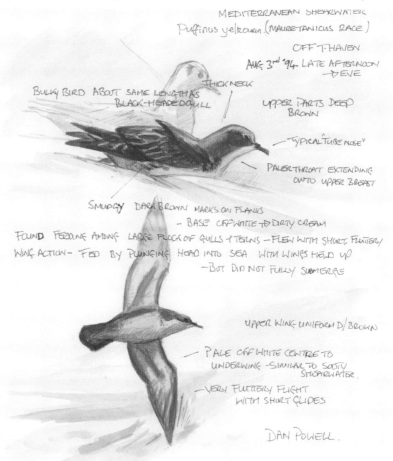

MEDITERRANEAN SHEARWATER
Puffinus yelkouan (MAURETANICUS RACE)
OFF T.HAVEN
AUG 3rd '94 LATE AFTERNOON
→ EVE
THICK NECK
BULKY BIRD ABOUT SAME LENGTH AS BLACK-HEADED GULL
UPPER PARTS DEEP BROWN
"TYPICAL TUBE NOSE"
PALER THROAT EXTENDING ONTO UPPER BREAST
SMUDGY DARK BROWN MARKS ON FLANKS
- BASE OFF WHITE → DIRTY CREAM
FOUND FEEDING AMONG LARGE FLOCK OF GULLS & TERNS — FLEW WITH SHORT FLUTTERY WING ACTION — FED BY PLUNGING HEAD INTO SEA WITH WINGS HELD UP
— BUT DID NOT FULLY SUBMERGE
UPPER WING UNIFORM D/ BROWN
— PALE OFF WHITE CENTRE TO UNDERWING — SIMILAR TO SOOTY SHEARWATER.
— VERY FLUTTERY FLIGHT WITH SHORT GLIDES
DAN POWELL.

During the afternoon of 3rd August **1995** a flock of 17 **Cormorants** was observed circling high over the reserve.

4th On 4th August **1996** a **Sparrowhawk** was observed taking a Common Sandpiper on the South Scrape.

A gathering of 9 **Dunnocks** feeding together below the feeders within the grounds of the visitor centre on 4th August **2008** was very unusual, for a species normally observed alone outside the breeding season.

5th A recently fledged **Cuckoo** was being fed by a **Lesser Whitethroat** close to the Meon Shore hide on 5th August **1991**.

6th Two **Swallow** nestlings ringed in the same nest at Old Netley on 6th August **1988**, were both caught thirty-one days later in a reed-bed roost at the Haven on the evening of 6th September.

The North Scrape June 2004 (Barry Duffin)

7th An adult **White-rumped Sandpiper** on the South Scrape from 7th to 18th August **1995** was the third record for the Haven.

8th A record number of 34 **Green Sandpipers** were counted on 8th August **1997**. The majority of these birds were feeding at Upper Haven, on marshy ground that had recently been disturbed as a result of excavation works.

9th Hampshire's first **Little Bittern** since 1869 was an immature bird at the Haven on 9th August **1953**. The bird was watched from the harbour bridge as it basked in full sunshine at 0800 hrs.

10th The highest ever autumn reed-bed roost of **Sand Martins** in Hampshire was of 3,500 birds at the Haven on 10th August **1977**.

11th A count of 21 **Common Sandpipers** at the Haven on the evening of 11th August **1981** is yet to be surpassed..

12th A **Melodious Warbler** observed from along the eastern boardwalk on 12th August **1978** was the first for the reserve and only the eighth Hampshire record. That evening 3 **Black Terns** feeding in the South Scrape attracted the attention of a so-called television celebrity, who found it necessary to trespass into the reserve. He was escorted off the site after being found on the grass bank in front of the Meon Shore hide.

13th A male **Common Rosefinch** in Titchfield on 13th August **1913** remains the only Hampshire record of this eastern vagrant.

14th A **Sedge Warbler** ringed on its wintering grounds 4054 km to the south in Senegal on 19th December 1991, was recaptured at the Haven on 14th August **1992**.

A juvenile **Purple Heron** was seen to arrive from the south and to drop into riverside reeds at about 1230 hrs on 14th August **1994**. The bird was later watched flying around the North Scrape before disappearing into the Eleven Acre Mere.

70

15th The one thousandth **Grasshopper Warbler** to be ringed at the Haven was on 15th August **2006**.

16th A flock of 7 **Wood Sandpipers** that left the scrapes in a westerly direction on the evening of 16th August **2004** is one of the two highest counts made in the County.

17th One of the highest counts of **Turtle Doves** on the reserve is of 12 on 17th August **1988**.

Turtle Dove (Dennis Bright)

18th A juvenile **White-winged Black Tern** on 18th August **1971** was the first record for the Haven and the seventh for Hampshire.

19th During an early morning ringing session on 19th **August 2006** two **Aquatic Warblers** were caught. One of these birds was subsequently retrapped nine days later 394 km to the south in southwest France. This was only the second recovery abroad of a British ringed Aquatic Warbler. The first having been a bird ringed at Radipole Lake, Dorset, the day before the Haven bird, and retrapped 234 km to the south in France on 19th August.

Two Aquatic Warblers 19th August 2006 (Barry Duffin)

Little Egret from Suffern Hide (Barry Duffin)

Pochard and Tufted Duck flighting in to feeding station (Dennis Bright)

20th The fledging of two **Ringed Plover** chicks on the scrapes on 20th August 1994, was the first and only successful rearing within the Haven.

21st The largest single flock of **Crossbills** recorded at the Haven is of 12 flying west on 21st August **1988**.

22nd A juvenile **Ortolan Bunting** was on the edge of farmland on the western side of the reserve on 22nd August **1984**.

On the morning of 22nd August **2004** 189 **Sedge Warblers** were ringed.

Seventy-four **Grasshopper Warblers** being ringed in the early hours of 22nd August **2009** was an exceptional total.

23rd The highest day count of **Arctic Terns** is of 100 on 23rd August **1993**.

24th During a torrential rainstorm around midday on 24th August **1984** a flock of 28 **Curlew Sandpipers** arrived on the South Scrape. The birds remained some forty minutes before departing.

25th The first occurrence of a **Nightjar** at the Haven was on 25th August **1956**.

A **Kingfisher** ringed as a juvenile on 26th August **1975** was found shot seventeen days later at Locks Heath, near Warsash.

26th A pair of **Bearded Tits** were still feeding young in a nest on 26th August **1988**

Bearded Tit (Nigel Harland)

27th A juvenile **Sedge Warbler** ringed on 27th August **1973** was found dead in Ghana, 4,480 km to the south on 3rd August 1974. This was the first finding of a British ringed Sedge Warbler in that country.

At about 1120 hrs on the 27th August **1996** an adult **Squacco Heron** was observed in the lower Haven. The bird remained in the area until the evening when it was seen to fly off south towards the Isle of Wight at 1720 hrs. This was the third Hampshire record and the second for the Haven.

28th An exceptionally high count of 33 **Whinchats** occurred on 28th August **1977**.

The highest count of **Grey Herons** on the reserve is of 22 on 28th August **1981**.

A juvenile **Sand Martin** ringed at an evening reed-bed roost at the Haven on 28th August **1990**, was retrapped and released in the Parc National du Djoudi, Senegal on 8th March 1991.

A **Blue-winged Teal** discovered on 28th August **2009**, on the Eleven Acre Mere, was only the sixth Hampshire record of this North American duck.

29th An immature **Red-necked Grebe** was offshore for the second day on 29th August **1996**.

28/8/96 - 12.00
JUV. RED-NECKED GREBE FEEDING
OFF SEAWALL · VERY SURPRISED
WHEN COMMON
SEAL
SURFACED
ALONG SIDE IT

YELLOWISH
BILL

NB — JUVENILE STRIPES ON
CHEEKS
DULL ORANGE
NECK.

30th During a ringing session in the reed-beds on 30th August **1993** a **Spotted Crake** approached the ringers who were able to drop a net over it.

Spotted Crake
August 1993
(Barry Duffin)

31st A **Swallow** ringed as a juvenile on 31st August **1976** was a road casualty 9280 km to the south in Cape Town, South Africa on 14th November 1981.

A juvenile male **Firecrest** trapped and ringed on 31st August **2002** was the earliest autumn returning bird recorded at the Haven.

A **Wheatear** of the sub-species *Oenanthe oenanthe leucorrhoa*, the Greenland Wheatear, was ringed on the morning of 31st August **2008**. Also on 31st August 2008 three **Marsh Harriers** and an **Osprey** put on a spectacular aerial display as they met over the river.

Osprey close to Suffern hide (Dennis Bright)

September

With the harvesting of cereals now complete, hundreds of Canada Geese can be attracted to the stubble on nearby farmland. In the reserve the river offers sanctuary to these birds overnight or when put to flight during daylight hours. Large numbers of Rooks and Jackdaws will also begin to feed on the farmland during the month. Flocks can be seen flying westwards over the Haven soon after dawn, returning in the late afternoon and evening when heading for their roost site on the Gosport side of Portsmouth harbour.

The southward migration of our summer visitors continues, and it is now the turn of Blackcaps and Chiffchaffs, that pass through the reserves woodland and scrub areas in their hundreds. Many Chiffchaffs will often be heard singing at this time of year from the canopy of the sallows and oaks, whilst Blackcaps will be found feeding on blackberries in the hedgerows and patches of bramble. It is worth scanning the roadside bushes for perching Whinchats, Stonechats, Wheatears and the occasional Dartford Warbler at this time of year.

1st During gale force south-westerly winds and heavy rain on 1st September **1992,** a **Manx Shearwater** was observed from the Spurgin hide as it flew high over the Haven in an easterly direction.

An **Osprey** was observed fishing close to the harbour bridge on 1st September **1997.**

On 1st September **2002** a juvenile **Bluethroat** was trapped and ringed in the early morning at Upper Haven. This was the sixth record for the reserve.

Juvenile Bluethroat 1st September 2002 (Barry Duffin)

2nd A **Melodious Warbler** at the Haven on 2nd September **1963** was only the second County record.

A female **Blackcap** ringed on 2nd September **1990** was found dead 1743 km to the south in Morocco on 6th March 1995.

3rd The largest autumn passage of **Sand Martins** witnessed in the County is of 2,000 flying south at the Haven on 3rd September **1961.**

On 3rd September **1966** a female **Little Bittern** was flushed from the riverside. This was the fourth record at the Haven.

A **Cetti's Warbler** ringed on 3rd September **2004** was retrapped 193 km to the west in south Devon on 30th January 2005. This remains the furthest known movement of a Cetti's Warbler originating from the Haven.

4th An early autumn migrating juvenile female **Merlin** was trapped and ringed on 4th September **1986**.

Juvenile female Merlin
September 1986
(Barry Duffin)

5th In clear skies and a light southerly wind a **Honey Buzzard** flew out over the Solent on 5th September **1986**. The second record for the reserve.

A **Jack Snipe** on 5th September **1990** was the second earliest County record for an autumn returning bird.

6th An autumn reed-bed roost of 555 **Yellow Wagtails** on 6th September **1973** is the highest ever recorded in Hampshire.

7th A flock of 21 **Greenshanks** observed flying down river at 0800 hrs on 7th September **1988**, continued their journey out over the Solent.

8th A **Hoopoe** was observed in the meadows on the west side of the river on the afternoon of 8th September **1956**.

9th An adult **Common Sandpiper** ringed on 28th May 1974, was found dead 1884 km to the north-east in northern Sweden on 9th September **1979**.

10th A female **Sparrowhawk** was seen taking a Jay on the lawn of Haven Cottage on 10th September **2004**.

11th The second highest autumn reed-bed roost of **Yellow Wagtails** is of 520 on 11th September **1969**.

12th An **Osprey** observed flying down river and out over the sea at 0900 hrs on 12th September **2002**, was followed by another at 1200 hrs.

13th One of the largest gatherings of **Rooks** was on 13th September **1986** when 200+ birds fed in the east meadows.

14th A **Wilson's Phalarope** in juvenile plumage appeared on the South Scrape during the afternoon of 14th September **1989**. This was the first occurrence of this North American wader at the Haven and the fourth to occur in Hampshire. The bird was still present the next day.

15th After a large overnight arrival of migrants a **Wryneck** was ringed on the morning of 15th September **1974**. This was the first record for the Haven.

The presence of 19 **Stonechats** on 15th September **1995** suggested that these were newly arrived migrants.

The highest day count of **Common Buzzards** is of 16 on 15th September **2007**. The majority of these birds were observed soaring over Upper Haven.

16th After a large overnight arrival of **Blackcaps** a record 136 birds were ringed on the morning of 16th September **2004**.

17th The first **Bluethroat** for the Haven was discovered on 17th September **1961**.

A **Peregrine Falcon** was observed taking a Turnstone as it flew over Hill Head harbour on 17th September **1995**.

18th Whilst watching over the eastern meadows on 18th September **1976**, several hundred Black-headed Gulls suddenly lifted into the air from the river as if spooked by a bird of prey. On looking up an adult **White Stork** was located soaring over the Frying Pan. The bird gradually lost height and looked to be aiming to land in the meadows but then almost immediately started to gain height and was observed to soar off westwards. This was the first record for the reserve.

Kingfisher (Dennis Bright)

81

A feeding flock of 80 **House Sparrows** in Marsh Lane on 18th September **1986** has been the highest day count for the reserve.

A **Honey Buzzard** was observed high over the Haven being mobbed by Carrion Crows on 18th September **1996**. This was only the fourth occurrence of this scarce passage migrant at the reserve.

19th A **Red-rumped Swallow** was observed from the roadside viewing platform as it flew low over the river with other hirundines on 19th September **1988**. The bird was seen independently about an hour later by another observer to the west side of the reserve. This was only the second record for Hampshire.

20th A **Moorhen** ringed at the Haven on 31st December 1983, was shot 201 km to the east near Calais, France on 20th September **1984**.

The highest count of roosting **Oystercatchers** on the scrapes is of 188 on 20th September **2005**.

Oystercatcher flock South Scrape (Dennis Bright)

21st An adult **Spotted Crake** found feeding on the South Scrape on 21st September **1997** remained until at least 5th October.

Only the second **Wryneck** to be ringed on the reserve was during the early morning of 21st September **2003**.

Wryneck September 2003
(Barry Duffin)

22nd A surprise visitor on the South Scrape on 22nd September **1983** was a **Citrine Wagtail**. This was the first occurrence in Hampshire of this eastern vagrant. A **Pectoral Sandpiper**, on the South Scrape earlier the same day, was also a first record for the reserve.

A **Grasshopper Warbler** ringed on 22nd September **2009** brought the season's total to an incredible 569 birds.

23rd The highest count of autumn passage **Little Stints** is of 21 on the scrapes on 23rd September **1996**.

An intermediate morph juvenile **Long-tailed Skua** first seen offshore on 23rd September **2007** was reported daily thereafter until 27th September.

24th With low water levels in the river at the end of a summer drought in **1976** record numbers of **Greenshanks** fed on exposed mud banks. A peak of 28 birds was recorded on 24th September.

Greenshanks on South Scrape (Dennis Bright)

Autumn migrating **Meadow Pipits** totalled 236 birds as they were counted heading out over the Solent in a south-easterly direction in fog on the morning of 24th September **2000**.

After the most successful breeding season on record for **Gadwall** at the Haven, a count of 98 was made on 24th September **2007**.

The highest count of **Canada Geese** is of 740 on 24th September **2008**.

25th The largest day count of autumn migrating **Swallows** witnessed at the Haven is of 30,000 moving west on 25th September **1958**.

The first sighting of an **Aquatic Warbler** at the Haven was on 25th September **1960**.

The annual autumn reed-bed roost of **Swallows** reached a peak of 5,500 birds on 25th September **1980**, the largest roost ever recorded in Hampshire.

84

River Meon and Duck Bay from the Suffern Hide August 1989 (Barry Duffin)

River Meon and Duck Bay from Suffern Hide January 2000 (Barry Duffin)

A Juvenile **House Martin** ringed in Strathclyde, Scotland on 28th August 1986, was trapped at the Haven on 25th September **1986**. This has been one of only two long distance recoveries involving birds retrapped in Hampshire.

26th The earliest autumn record of **Water Pipit** is of 2 on 26th September 1993.

27th The highest count of **Spotted Redshanks** on the reserve is of 14 on 27th September **1986**.

28th A **Raven** observed over Posbrook Meadows on 28th September **1999** flew high to the south-east. This was only the second record for the Haven.

A **Wren** ringed at the Haven on 28th September **2002** was found freshly dead 68 km to the east at Shoreham-by-Sea, Sussex on 10th December 2002.

29th A flock of 12 **Lesser Redpolls** was ringed in the garden of Haven Cottage on 29th September **1974**. Only fourteen have been ringed since.

The first sighting of a **Yellow-legged Gull** at the Haven was of an adult on 29th September **1981**.

An immature/female **Montagu's Harrier** flew west over farmland to the west of the reserve on 29th September **2005**. This remains the only occurrence of this scarce bird of prey in the Titchfield Haven area.

The fourteenth **Aquatic Warbler** to be ringed at the Haven was on 29th September **2007**.

30th A juvenile male **Bluethroat** was trapped and ringed on 30th September **1962**. This was the third Haven record.

During an unprecedented influx of **Honey Buzzards** into the country, 7 birds were recorded on 30th September **2000** at the Haven.

October

Some of the autumn's long distance travellers are now beginning to arrive in the Solent where they will be spending the winter. Brent Geese have made the journey from the Russian Arctic tundra, Wigeon and Teal from east of the Baltic, and Black-tailed Godwits from Iceland.

Early October is the best time to observe the Haven's Bearded Tits. For much of the year they remain elusive, whilst feeding in dense reed-beds, but following their post-breeding moult in August and September they become more adventurous. Birds may be seen flying high over the lower Haven in small parties for short periods before dropping almost vertically back into bushes and reeds. Some will be heading off eastwards for marshes in Kent or East Anglia for the winter whilst others will remain at the Haven.

Flocks of Scandinavian Redwing and Fieldfare will be arriving in the country during the month but few are likely to be observed at the Haven until later in the winter. However when listening outside on a clear moonlight night, the thin 'see-ip' calls of many Redwing may be heard passing over as they head further south.

1st A flock of 75 **Jays** flew west at 0840 hrs, closely followed by a smaller flock of 20 birds on 1st October **1975**. Many of these birds were noted carrying acorns in their bills.

A **Nightjar** was ringed and released on the evening of 1st October **1976**. The following year another Nightjar was again found on the late date of 1st October. On this occasion the bird had died after being hit by a road vehicle during the previous night.

The earliest sighting of an autumn returning **Brambling** is of one on 1st October **1996**.

Hampshire's first **Paddyfield Warbler** was trapped and ringed at the Haven at 0705 hrs on 1st October **2000**. Later that morning yet another Hampshire first at the Haven, was a North American **Cliff Swallow** that appeared over the river at approximately 1030 hrs feeding among several hundred **House Martins**.

Paddyfield Warbler 1st October 2000 (Trevor Codlin)

2nd A **Tawny Pipit** was found feeding on the banks of the South Scrape at midday on 2nd October **1988**. Later that afternoon an adult **White-rumped Sandpiper** was discovered on the edge of the river opposite the Suffern hide at approximately 1345 hrs. This bird remained until 5th October.

88

Following an oil spillage at the Fawley Oil Refinery, 105 **Teal** observed at the Haven in the week beginning 2nd October **1989** showed signs of having oiled plumage.

It is rare to observe an **Aquatic Warbler** in the field, but one showed well in vegetation below the Meon Shore hide on 2nd October **1993**.

3rd The highest count of **Bearded Tits** on a single day is of 40 on 3rd October **1993**.

4th On 4th October **1976** at 1015 hrs a **Honey Buzzard** was watched soaring over the scrapes before heading out southwards. This was the first record for the Haven.

The ring from a **Common Snipe** ringed at the Haven on 4th October **1979** was found in a **Peregrine Falcon's** nest 2464 km to the north-east in northern Finland on 20th August 1980.

On the 4th October **1986** a **Spotted Sandpiper** was discovered feeding on the South Scrape. The bird remained until 12th January 1987. This was the first occurrence in Hampshire of this North American wader.

Spotted Sandpiper on South Scrape October 1986 (Barry Duffin)

A **Yellow-browed Warbler** was found feeding in sallows just north of the Suffern Hide on 4th October **2005**. The fourth record for the reserve.

Eighty-three **Chiffchaffs** were ringed on the morning of 4th October **2006**.

5th Of 5 **Dunnocks** flying together over the lower Haven on 5th October **1987**, 3 eventually moved off to the east.

Forty-four **Goldcrests** were ringed on the morning of 5th October **2004** following a large overnight arrival.

6th A **Great White Egret** was observed feeding on the Frying Pan early on the morning of 6th October **2007**. The bird later visited waters in front of the Spurgin hide before eventually flying off westwards. This was the first record for the Haven.

Great White Egret from Spurgin hide October 2007 (John Dodds)

7th On 7th October **1980** a juvenile **Swallow** that had been ringed at the Haven on 1st September 1980, came on board a ship off the West African coast with other hirundines. Unfortunately the bird died a few days later. The ship was 5600 km to the south of the ringing site at the Haven.

8th A **Corncrake** was a surprise catch during a ringing session on 8th October **2000**. This was only the third Haven occurrence of this rare summer visitor.

Corncrake 8th October 2000 (Trevor Codlin)

A duck **Mallard** was in the harbour with a brood of ten newly hatched ducklings on 8th October **2007**.

9th The first occurrence of a **Lapland Bunting** at the Haven was on 9th October **1973**.

A **Nightingale** reported on 9th October **1983** was the latest ever sighting in Hampshire.

On the 9th October **1988** a juvenile **Pomarine Skua** was observed on flooded meadows close to the Frying Pan. When observers approached to within 25 metres of the bird in a tractor, it was found to be feeding on a gull carcass. Whilst being observed the bird frequently took flight and circled low over the meadow before returning to the gull. It remained in the area until at least 31st October.

A **Richard's Pipit** flew westwards over the lower Haven calling repeatedly during the morning of 9th October **1994**.

10th Flocks of sixteen and ten **Long-tailed Tits** left independently of each other on the morning of 10th October **1989** and flew off high to the west.

91

11th Whilst mist-netting on the morning of 11th October **1975** a **Cetti's Warbler** was caught. There had been no indication of the presence of the bird. This was the first Cetti's Warbler at the Haven since the first British record in 1961.

Between 0815 hrs and 1015 hrs on 11th October **1980,** 1,560 **Chaffinches** were counted flying westwards.

A **Yellow-browed Warbler** was found along the canal path on 11th October **1995**. This was followed by 2 birds in the same area on 15th October. These were the second and third records for the reserve.

12th A female Sparrowhawk was witnessed taking a **Woodpigeon** in the east meadows on 12th October **1984**.

13th On hearing the characteristic loud tacking call of a **Ring Ouzel**, a bird was located in sallows close to the Walkway Pond on 13th October **1993**.

14th The earliest autumn arriving **Black Redstart** was on 14th October **1995**.

Black Redstart
(Dennis Bright)

15th During the morning and afternoon of the 15th October **1981** 24,000 **House Martins** moved westwards. Between 1130 hrs and 1200 hrs 8,000 were counted. The movement slowed during the afternoon and birds began feeding low and in dense flocks. There were reports of many having been hit by cars. Several birds that were handled had considerable amounts of fat on them. This remains the largest day total of House Martins ever recorded in Hampshire.

A storm-driven **Fulmar** found on the footpath behind Haven House on 15th October **1983** was later released.

16th The first record for the Haven of a **Glaucous Gull** was of an adult bird on 16th October **1948**. This was only the second Hampshire record in the twentieth century after the first in 1921.

17th A **White-rumped Sandpiper** observed on the Frying Pan on 17th October **1963** was the first record of this North American wader in Hampshire.

At approximately 1445 hrs on 17th October **1986** a **Sociable Plover** was discovered feeding on an area of exposed mud at the southern end of the South Scrape. The bird associated with **Lapwings** and was aggressive towards them, and whilst in flight it would itself be harassed by them. Following the finding of the bird at the Haven on 17th, it was to put in only two more brief appearances on the reserve during its stay in the area. Most of the time from the 18th to 24th was spent on farmland to the west of the reserve, then from 25th October to 8th November it frequented HMS Daedalus airfield to the east of the reserve. This remains the only record of this species in Hampshire.

Sociable Plover South Scrape 17th October 1986 (Barry Duffin)

Following the severe hurricane force winds that struck the area on the night of 15th/16th October **1987** as many as 7 **Sabine's Gulls**, 3 adults and 4 juveniles, were observed offshore during the afternoon of 17th.

18th A **Razorbill** found dead on the shore on 18th October **1959**, had been ringed on 16th June 1959 at Cape Frechal, Cotes du Nord, France.

The highest autumn count of **Pied Wagtails** going to roost in riverside reed-beds is of 400+ birds on 18th October **1977**.

A **Jay** was observed planting acorns on the lawn at Haven Cottage on 18th October **1994**. During the course of observations nine acorns were regurgitated one at a time and buried in the ground.

19th Just after midday on 19th October **1988** three **Ring Ouzels** together with a single **Fieldfare** were seen dropping into the Haven from some considerable height and alighting in a row of oak trees.

20th At approximately 1105 hrs on 20th October **2006** a **Cory's Shearwater** was discovered sitting on the sea close inshore. The bird later flew off eastwards, passing close to the harbour. This was only the second ever sighting of the species off the Hampshire coast.

21st The last record of **Cirl Bunting** at the Haven was when 2 were observed in Marsh Lane on 21st October **1962**.

A **Purple Sandpiper** roosting with a flock of **Turnstones** at the lower end of the river on 21st October **1990** was only the second Haven record.

22nd A **Goldcrest** ringed at Portland Bill on 22nd October **2000** was retrapped at the Haven ten days later, on 1st November.

23rd The highest count of **Little Grebes** is of 17 on the river on 23rd October **1983**.

At approximately 1140 hrs on 23rd October **1990** the calls of one or more **Penduline Tits** were heard close to the Meon Shore hide. To the west of the hide a flock of 5 birds, calling frequently, were located among reeds. The flock eventually moved eastwards, and was lost from sight as they most probably crossed to the east side of the river. This was the third record for the reserve and similarly for Hampshire.

24th A **Lesser Yellowlegs** was discovered feeding on the South Scrape during the late morning on 23rd October **2005**. This was the first occurrence of this North American wader at the Haven. The bird remained until 28th October, being observed on occasions feeding within the flooded meadows below Titchfield village.

Lesser Yellowlegs South Scrape October 2005 (Gordon Small)

The calls of **Blackbirds**, **Song Thrushes** and **Redwing** were heard close to midnight on 24th October **2002** when large numbers of thrushes were passing overhead.

25th The latest date for **Osprey** at the Haven is of a single bird on 25th October **1976**.

A first winter **Hen Harrier** observed hunting over the upper reserve on 25th October **2006** was seen to be carrying identifiable wing-tags. Subsequent enquiries showed that the bird was one of a brood of 5 young that had fledged from a nest in the Peak District, Derbyshire during the previous summer.

26th A **Pallas's Warbler** was found to the west of the reserve at Thatcher's Copse on 26th October **1988**. This was only the second occurrence of this Siberian vagrant in Hampshire.

27th A drake **American Wigeon** was located during the afternoon of 27th October **1978** on the North Scrape, among a flock of 120 **Wigeon**. This bird was considered to be the first truly wild bird for the Haven, and the second County record.

A **Blackcap** ringed on 27th October **2007** brought the total of this species ringed during the year to a record seven hundred and four.

Two **Ravens** were attracted to the carcass of a cow in the western meadows on 27th October **2007** within hours of the animal dying.

28th During an autumn movement of passerines 540 **Tree Sparrows** and 567 **Greenfinches** were counted flying westwards on 28th October 1961.

A flock of 14 **Velvet Scoters** offshore on 28th October 1985 was seen to fly off westwards after being disturbed by pilot whales.

Two **Penduline Tits** first located on call, were observed flying over westwards on 28th October 1989. This was the first record for Hampshire.

29th The reserve's first record of a **Purple Sandpiper** was on 29th October 1983, when a bird was discovered roosting on a groyne in the harbour.

The only record of **Red-throated Pipit** in Hampshire is of a single bird that was watched feeding on the south scrape on the 29th October 1989.

A party of 3 calling **Crossbills** observed coming in from the east on 29th October 1997, circled and came down to drink at a pool, before eventually continuing their flight westwards.

30th On the 30th October 1977 a flock of 30 **Blue Tits** was seen to fly high to the west.

A **Siberian Stonechat** of the race either *Saxicola torquata maura* or *stejnegeri* was feeding from tops of reeds in the mid-marsh reed-beds on 30th October 1988.

31st During the afternoon of 31st October 1974 in clear skies a **Rough-legged Buzzard** soared over the reserve before heading off westwards.

The latest date for a **Reed Warbler** on the reserve is the 31st October 1987.

November

The majority of the reserve's wintering species of wildfowl are now present although having not reached their peak numbers. If the autumn has been a wet one, then much of the valley grassland will be showing surface water, particularly the meadows immediately below Titchfield village. This in turn may attract large numbers of Lapwing, Black-tailed Godwits, Common Snipe, Teal and Shoveler. The area has on occasions been a favourite haunt of Water Pipits.

Small numbers of Tufted Duck and Pochard will now be joining Mallard and Coot at the evening feeding station. Another evening activity now being regularly witnessed is the flighting in from the sea of a number of Cormorants that are heading for riverside willows where they will be roosting overnight.
Local Tawny Owls are often very vocal at night at this time of year as young birds begin establishing territories.

Reed Buntings are usually frequent visitors at this time of year to the feeders put out at the visitor centre. The nearby hedges provide cover for these birds and for the many finches and tits that may accompany them when disturbed.

1st Over 100 **Blackbirds** were present in the southeast area of the reserve on 1st November **1974** following a large overnight arrival.

2nd A **Great Grey Shrike** observed near the Meon Shore hide on 2nd November **1990** eventually flew out southwest towards Calshot, pursued by a **Pied Wagtail**.

A **Chiffchaff** ringed at the Haven on 2nd November **1991** was found in northern Spain almost nine years later on 15th October 2000.

3rd Little of any significance has been noted on this date.

4th At approximately 1245 hrs on 4th November **1982** a **Long-billed Dowitcher** was discovered on the South Scrape. The bird fed with several **Common Snipe** in tussocks of rank grass along the shoreline of the scrape, only occasionally wading into the nearby water to briefly feed, bathe and preen. The bird had earlier flown in from the east, calling as it passed over staff working along the visitor boardwalk. This was the fifth County record and the first for the reserve.

A party of 4 **Penduline Tits** was found at 1030 hrs on 4th November **1994** feeding on the seed heads of reed mace before departing high to the west at 1245 hrs. This was the fifth record for Hampshire.

5th Westerly movements of **Woodpigeons** often occur during the month of November. The largest movement so far recorded was of 8400 moving west north-west in one and a half hours on 5th November **1959**.

The highest number of **Little Auks** observed offshore on a single day is of 7 on 5th November **1998**.

6th On the 6th November **1986** a **Cattle Egret** was observed flying down river in the late afternoon at 1600 hrs. The bird was found to have gone to roost in willows on the edge of the Frying Pan. It was later learnt that a local farmer had seen a small white egret in with his sheep in meadows below Titchfield village two days earlier. This bird remained in the area until at least 11th January 1987, frequenting the same grazed pastures where first reported. On occasions later in the winter the bird was located feeding among grazing cattle at Warsash.

Cattle Egret November 1986 (Barry Duffin)

A male **Reed Bunting** ringed in Belgium on 6th November **1990** was recaptured 468 km to the west at the Haven on 16th February 1991.

7th A group of three **Whooper Swans** observed arriving from the west on 7th November **1981** flew on up river until out of sight.

8th A drake **Green-winged Teal**, first discovered on 8th November **1998**, remained at least until mid November. Most likely it was the same individual that reappeared in mid December and remained until 2nd January 1999.

9th On 9th November **1989** a **Penduline Tit** was trapped and ringed in the reed-bed in front of Haven Cottage. The second record for the reserve and the County.

Penduline Tit 9th November 1989 (Barry Duffin)

99

On the 9th November **2000** a party of 5 **Shore Larks** was watched coming in off the sea and landing briefly on the beach. They then departed to the north-west and were not seen again. The first record for the Haven.

A **Cetti's Warbler** ringed on 9th November **2000**, brought the total ringed in the year to one hundred.

10th In the late afternoon on 10th November **1999**, as wildfowl gathered on the river at the evening feeding station, a **Ferruginous Duck** was identified among them.

11th A ringtail **Hen Harrier** was hunting over the upper marsh on 11th November **2004**, and was thought to have later gone to roost in nearby reed-beds.

12th On 12th November **2007**, a **Little Auk** first discovered offshore, later flew off northwards.

13th A male and a female **Black Redstart** were feeding among the beach huts on 13th November **1984**.

14th A drake **Mallard** shot close to Titchfield village on 14th November **1983** had been ringed 1117 km to the east in Poland on 24th June 1982.

15th The first **Rough-legged Buzzard** recorded at the Haven was on 15th November **1959**. On this occasion the bird was accompanied by a **Marsh Harrier**.

16th The latest occurrence of an autumn **Wheatear** at the Haven is of a single bird on 16th November **1975**.

17th The highest count of **Feral Pigeons** is of 762 on 17th November **1997**.

18th Only 2 **Coal Tits** have been ringed on the reserve, the last being on 18th November **2005** and the first on 26th December 2001.

Coal Tit (Barry Duffin)

19th A single **Sand Martin** over the river on 19th November **2004** was the latest ever sighting in Hampshire. The bird was trapped and ringed later that day.

20th At least 21 different **Water Rails** were located on call at dusk in the mid-marsh reed-beds region of the reserve on 20th November **2005**.

21st Three **Twite** observed on 21st November **1959** was only the second occurrence of this rare winter visitor to the site. There have only been four records since.

22nd A **Snow Bunting** frequented the South Scrape and the roadside during the early morning of 22nd November **1975**.

23rd An escaped **Chilean Flamingo** was present from 23rd November **2003** until at least 16th April 2004.

24th The daily autumn feeding movement of **Rooks** and **Jackdaws** numbered almost 1000 birds soon after first light on 24th November **1999** as mixed flocks headed for farmland to the west of the reserve. Late in the afternoon birds returned eastwards to roost in woodland four miles away on the edge of Portsmouth Harbour.

25th On the 25th November **2000** a **Grey Phalarope** frequented the North Scrape during a period of rough weather.

26th The largest flock of **Stock Doves** is of 320 on 26th November **1978**. The birds were observed feeding in the eastern meadows.

A **Goldcrest** found trapped in a spider's web in a neighbouring garden on 26th November **1987**, was later released alive and well after being untangled.

A **Red Kite** being mobbed by **Carrion Crows** near Brownwich Pond on 26th November **1990** slowly headed east and arrived at the Haven ten minutes later, where it was observed for some time before eventually flying off in a north-easterly direction.

A freshly dead **Little Auk** was picked up in the yacht-club car park on 26th November **1999** during a period of gale force winds.

27th A **Hawfinch** observed near the Suffern hide on 27th November **1980** flew off westwards. This was the Haven's first record of this rare visitor.

28th A **Black Redstart** was watched catching insects in the grounds and from the roof of the visitor centre on 28th November **1994**.

29th A **Marsh Harrier** was observed walking around on the grass banks of the scrapes on 29th November **1990** during the late morning.

A **Leach's Petrel** which had been found on a car transporting cargo vessel in Southampton Docks on 29th November **1991**, was released into the sea at 1640 hrs the next morning at the Haven.

30th One of the highest counts of **Bullfinches** is of 12 on 30th November **2005**.

Brent Geese in east meadows November 2008 (Barry Duffin)

December

By the beginning of December wintering Bitterns have usually taken up residence within the marshes. It is often difficult to assess the number present due to their secretive nature, but often at least two to three individuals can be involved. Birds are regularly seen flighting over the riverside reed-beds when viewed from either the Suffern hide or the Knights Bank hide, particularly on mornings following heavy overnight frosts.

In cold weather the reserve's Barn Owls may be forced to hunt for longer hours and if so they will be seen hunting over the meadows in the early morning or late afternoon. The canal path makes an ideal vantage point from which to view these birds when they visit the adjacent water meadows. December is also a time when wintering Chiffchaffs and the occasional Firecrest can be found feeding in sheltered positions along the canal banks.

1st On 1st December **1978** a **Yellow-browed Warbler** was found feeding in riverside sallows south of the Suffern hide. The bird remained until 1st January 1979. This was the first record for the reserve and only the third for Hampshire.

2nd A **Great Skua** offshore on 2nd December **2007** is only the fourth record for that month at the Haven.

3rd One of the highest counts of **Red-breasted Mergansers** is of 30 offshore on 3rd December **1961**.

4th A **Blue Tit** ringed on 29th September 1974 was recaptured at Portland Bill on 4th December **1975**.

Some twelve thousand four hundred **Starlings** were counted flying eastwards across the reserve towards their overnight roost site in pines close to the Swordfish public house on 4th December **1983**.

5th A flock of 16 **White-fronted Geese** observed feeding on nearby farmland on 5th December **1991** later moved into the reserve where they remained until the last days of February.

Evening feeding station December 1997 (Barry Duffin)

6th A single **Turtle Dove** on 6th December **1966** is one of the latest records of this species in Hampshire.

7th A **Spotted Crake** was seen to flying from the western meadows to the canal path on 7th December **1987**. The bird was located in grass close to the footpath and was watched down to a distance of fifteen feet before it flew across the canal and into reeds.

Whilst a work party was in progress on 7th December **1996** a **Red Kite** was observed flying high overhead at approximately 1130 hrs.

8th A late **Yellow Wagtail** on 8th December **1957** was possibly a wintering bird.

Whilst a count was being taken of **Pied Wagtails** coming in to roost in reed-beds on the evening of 8th December **1985**, a **Sparrowhawk** was seen to fly low over the roost taking a bird.

9th A flock of at least 1000 **Brent Geese** were feeding on autumn sown cereals in the field behind the east boundary hedgerow on 9th December **1996**.

10th On the 10th December **1973** a record number of 2,140 **Teal** were counted. Some 1,960 birds flighted in from the south west between 1300 hrs and 1400 hrs. A feature of the winter had been the regular tidal movements to and from Southampton Water.

Drake Teal South Scrape (Dennis Bright)

11th A drake **Long-tailed Duck** which had been present since 11th December **1982** was joined by a duck on 18th December. Both then frequented the scrapes and the river until 28th April 1983.

12th A flock of 25 **Goldfinches** was feeding among alders near the Suffern hide on 12th December **1986**.

13th A female **Brambling** was found feeding in a field of sprouts close to Hammond's Bridge on the evening of 13th December **1985**.

14th A **Sedge Warbler** trapped and ringed on 14th December **1996** was still present the next day. This is the latest ever occurrence in Hampshire.

15th The highest count of **Goosanders** is of 9 redheads that flew over the reserve in a north-westerly direction on 15th December **1973**.

During a period when over 1000 **Brent Geese** had been feeding on cereal crops just to the west of the reserve, two were shot with the knowledge of the farm tenant on 15th December **1985**.

A **Bearded Tit** ringed on 15th December **1996** brought the total ringed for the year to 79 birds.

Male Bearded Tit
(Peter Dodsworth)

16th A first winter male **Gadwall** ringed at the Haven on 16th December **1986** was shot 236 km east on 2nd September 1987 in France. Only ten individuals of this species have been ringed on the reserve.

17th A **Red-necked Grebe** with oiled plumage that was observed on the river on 17th December **1996**, remained until at least 21st December.

18th A **Common Snipe** ringed at the Haven on 5th March 1979 was shot 208 km to the east in France on 18th December **1983**.

Common Snipe (Dennis Bright)

19th A flock of 8 **Pink-footed Geese** found feeding in water meadows below Titchfield village on 19th December **1987**, remained until 10th March 1988.

20th A **Barn Owl** was hunting over the water meadows on 20th December **2008**. The bird appeared took little notice of the observer, as it perched on a nearby fence post.

21st A female **Peregrine** observed in the east meadows during the afternoon of 21st December **1987** spent much of its time perched on a straw bale, and on at least two occasions flew down to the nearby river's edge to bathe.

22nd The first **American Wigeon** in Hampshire was at the Haven on 22nd December **1963**. It was considered that this bird was one of three that had earlier escaped from a collection in Portsmouth.

A **Swallow** on 22nd December **1977** is one of the latest County records for this species.

The last sighting of the once common **Corn Bunting** in the Haven was of a flock of 10 on 22nd December **1987**. Birds continued to be recorded on the Chilling farmland to the west of the reserve until April 1993.

23rd Five **Long-tailed Ducks** were offshore on 23rd December **1981**.

Four **Bitterns** were in the vicinity of the South Scrape on 23rd December **1983**, whilst a fifth bird was spotted in the northern region of the reserve. Three of the birds were in the reeds below the Meon Shore hide, one being seen to walk up the grassy bank close to the hide windows much to the amazement of observers within.

24th During a period of strong westerly winds on 24th December **1989** a **Leach's Petrel** flew up river at 1110 hrs, and then on its return journey down river was taken by a Sparrowhawk.

Marsh Harrier (Dennis Bright)

25th Two **Marsh Harriers**, including the regular bird, were observed soaring over the upper marsh reed-beds during the late morning of 25th December **1990**.

26th A first winter plumage **Ring-billed Gull** was observed in the lower end of the river during the morning of 26th December **1983**. This was the first record of this North American gull at the Haven and the fourth for Hampshire. The bird remained in the area until 19th February 1984, often frequenting playing fields in Stubbington Village.

27th At least 12 **Chiffchaffs** were feeding among sallows close to the Suffern hide on 27th December **2001**. One of these birds showing characteristics of the race of **Siberian Chiffchaff** *Phylloscopus collybita tristis* was trapped and ringed later in the day.

28th On 28th December **1993** a single **Common Crane** was seen flying west offshore.

Mallard gathering at the evening feeding station (Barry Duffin)

Red-throated Divers are usually observed offshore, so it was surprising to find a bird feeding on the river on 28th December **2001**.

29th A **Sparrowhawk** was watched flying low over the east meadows flushing and pursuing Common Snipe on 29th December **1995**.

30th The highest count of **Corn Buntings** has been of 90 going to roost in reed-beds at dusk on 30th December **1973**.

On the evening of 30th December **1977** a powerful torch was used to deflect **Wigeon** away from shooters who had lined up on the Upper Haven boundary. This followed several nights of indiscriminate shooting of the duck as they made their regular dusk flight up river.

During severe cold weather from December 1995 to February 1996 several hundred **Teal** fed on wheat put out on the lawn in front of Haven Cottage. The duck peaked at 470 on 30th December **1995**.

A wintering **Wheatear** discovered along the shore to the west of the reserve on 30th December 1994, was still present on 8th January **1995**.

31st During a period of heavy snowfall on 31st December **1961** 37,000 **Skylarks** were recorded moving eastwards, 33,000 of which moved in the period 0730 hrs to 1030 hrs.

Following overnight snowfalls large numbers of **Lapwing** were observed moving out southwards on 31st December **1978**. The majority of the birds were flying down Southampton Water. Many however were moving down the Meon Valley, and periodically, resting flocks built up in the reserve. Almost 6,000 birds were counted heading southwards during the day, whilst another 3,000 remained in the meadows in the late afternoon. On the same day 22,000 **Starlings** moved westwards in three hours watching.

Duck Bay 1976 (Barry Duffin)

The Haven in flood 2000 (David Pitt)

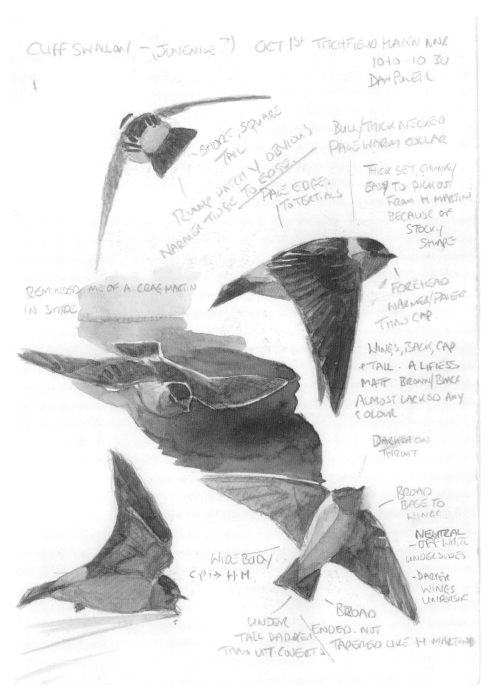

CLIFF SWALLOW - (JUVENILE ?) OCT 1st TITCHFIELD HAVEN NNR
10 to 10 30
DAN POWELL

- SHORT, SQUARE TAIL
RUMP PATCH V. OBVIOUS
WARMER TINGE TO EDGE.
PALE EDGES TO TERTIALS

BULL/THICK NECKED
PALE WARM COLLAR

THICK SET, CHUNKY
EASY TO PICK OUT
FROM H. MARTIN
BECAUSE OF
STOCKY
SHAPE

REMINDS ME OF A CRAG MARTIN
IN SHAPE

FOREHEAD
WARMER/PALER
THAN CAP.

WINGS, BACK, CAP
+ TAIL · A LIFELESS
MATT BROWN/BLACK
ALMOST LACKSO ANY
COLOUR.

DARKER ON
THROAT

BROAD
BASE TO
WINGS

NEUTRAL
- OFF WHITE
UNDERSIDES

- DARKER
WINGS
UNDERSIDE

WIDE BODY
CP. > H.M.

UNDER
TAIL DARKER
THAN U.T. COVERTS

BROAD
ENDED. NOT
TAPERED LIKE H. MARTINS

American Cliff Swallow 1st October 2000

112

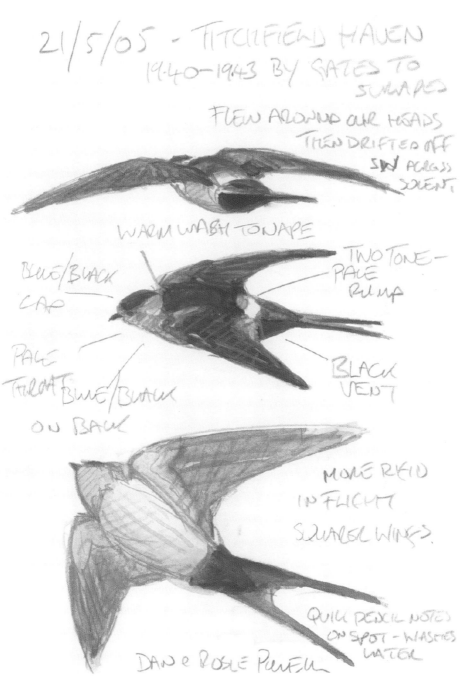

21/5/05 - TITCHFIELD HAVEN
19.40-19.43 BY GATES TO
SCRAPES

FLEW AROUND OUR HEADS
THEN DRIFTED OFF
SLW ACROSS
SOLENT

WARM WASH TO NAPE

BLUE/BLACK
CAP

TWO TONE -
PALE
RUMP

PALE
THROAT BLUE/BLACK
ON BACK

BLACK
VENT

MORE RED
IN FLIGHT
SQUARED WINGS.

QUICK PENCIL NOTES
ON SPOT - WASHES
LATER

DAN & ROSIE POWELL

Red-rumped Swallow 21st May 2005

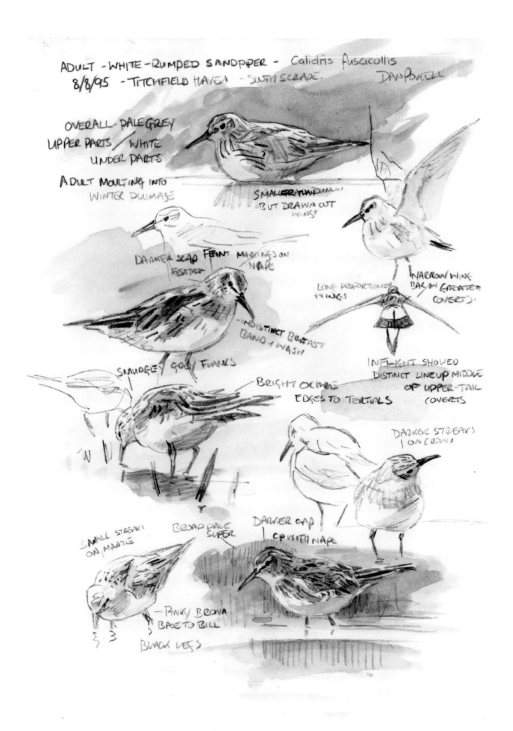

ADULT - WHITE - RUMPED SANDPPER - *Calidris fuscicollis*
8/8/95 - TITCHFIELD HAVEN - SOUTH SCRAPE.   DAN POWELL

OVERALL - PALE GREY
UPPER PARTS / WHITE
      UNDER PARTS

ADULT MOULTING INTO
      WINTER PLUMAGE

SMALLER THAN DUNLIN
BUT DRAWN OUT
      WINGS

DARKER SCAP FEINT MARKINGS ON
FEATHER   NAPE

LONG PROPORTIONED
      WINGS

NARROW WING
BAR ON GREATER
      COVERTS.

- INDISTINCT BREAST
BAND + WASH

SMUDGEY GREY FLANKS

BRIGHT OCHRE
EDGES TO TERTIALS

INFLIGHT SHOWED
DISTINCT LINE UP MIDDLE
      OF UPPER - TAIL
            COVERTS

DARKER STREAKS
ON CROWN

SMALL STREAKS
ON MANTLE

BROAD PALE
SUPER

DARKER CAP
CP WITH NAPE

- PINKY BROWN
BASE TO BILL

BLACK LEGS

White-rumped Sandpiper 8th August 1995

114

List of Observers

R A Andrews
J S Ash
M Ashton
G Barrett
D A Bell
E J Bennett
J K Bowers
C Brickwood
M Brickwood
D Bright
R Brown
M Bryant
I Calderwood
R J Carpenter
T Carpenter
P Carr
R A Chapman
R A Cheke
T D Codlin
J Coker
E Coleman
I Cox
C R Cuthbert
J R Davison
R H Dennis
J Dodds
P Dodsworth
K Douglas
B S Duffin
I S R Duffin
K Duffin
T M Duffin
R Dunn
P R Durnell
B J Friend
M Gibbons
R Gomes
G P Green

S Harthill
N Harland
L Hatfield
B A Heath
P Heath
M Hesk
M R Holmes
D Houghton
C Hopkins
M Howard
C Hughes
G Jones
N R Jones
R E Jones
R King
T A Lawman
H Langridge
R K Levett
R Lidstone-Scott
J Loveder
I Mac Pherson
A Madgewick
H Menhennet
L Morgan
P Morrison
S Morrison
J Moss
J Mozeley
A Y Norris
J A Norton
D Old
D Palmer
M J Palmer
J Parsons
D Pearce
M Pink
D Powell
K Powell

R Powell
E Pressey
D Price
P N Raby
B W Renyard
J Robertson
M A Rolfe
J Rogers
R Rogers
M Rose
S R Ruscoe
D Russell
A Savage
C Savage
N Schofield
A Searle
J Shephard
J R D Shillitoe
G Small
B Smith
L Smith
M D Smith
B Staples
J Staples
L Stride
C Suffern
J Switzer
M H Terry
V Thompson
W H Truckle
D Treacher
M Wagstaff
I Wells
D V Westerhoff
S L White
C Wilson
G Williams
E J Wiseman

It is acknowledged that many others not included in the list may also have been involved with observations included in this publication.

Species List